Behind the Facade

Behind the Facade

The Consulting Profession in Focus

Cautionary words for the wise

Lou Paris

Writer's Showcase
New York Lincoln Shanghai

Behind the Facade
The Consulting Profession in Focus

Writer's Showcase
an imprint of iUniverse, Inc.

For information address:
iUniverse
2021 Pine Lake Road, Suite 100
Lincoln, NE 68512
www.iuniverse.com

ISBN: 0-595-26810-2

Printed in the United States of America

The book is dedicated to the memory of three of my former colleagues

Giovanni Padovani, Michel Bosquet and Toni van Duijvendijk

Dear friends with whom I worked and enjoyed life for several years,
and with whom I enjoyed countless superb meals and the best vintage wines
in the "secret" restaurants we discovered throughout Europe.

Serve with dedication and courage
Respect truth and honesty,
The crown of integrity is never a burden
When your conscience is clear

P.Louis Bump, 1988

With special appreciation to Arnold F. Lessard my long-time friend and
Booz Allen Hamilton colleague for his editing contributions

CONTENTS

INTRODUCTION

Have you heard this before?

"Why should I use a consultant? Does he know more about my business than I do? I doubt it. Look at what happened to Adam when he took advice from the serpent. Anyway, isn't a consultant the guy who borrows your watch to tell you the time?"

It is natural for people to avoid exposing themselves to criticism, especially to troublesome criticism that might cause a change in their comfortable way of working and thinking. With this in mind, you may understand why managers can dig up a myriad of reasons for sticking solely with the use of internal resources to solve problems, and for developing purely internal perspective on markets, competition and technology. You can also imagine the limits to this perspective.

Another argument goes like this. "After all, why should a consultant, who provides services to troubled companies, be able to bring us better concepts, or ideas from those companies? He is working for clients with problems we don't have—and, besides, we know all about our business, our technologies, our processes and the new markets here and in the rest of the world—don't we? We read the trade journals, Business week and the Wall Street Journal! We are informed. Besides, consultants are expensive, too expensive for our tight budget. We're trying to find new markets, struggling to bring on new products, working to drive costs down and bring quality up, so we can be more competitive. We are swamped with these things, right now. Paying fees for a consultant would tear up our budget at a time when we need the money to hire more staff people to handle this temporary work overload."

Yes, these are samples of the conventional *wisdom* on consultants heard in many small and medium size companies. There are, on the other hand, large and small companies with broader perspective, and these companies measure their operating and strategic needs carefully, weigh them against the internal resources available and focus on satisfying the differences—many times by hiring consultants.

The recent, well-publicised, scandals involving large corporations and their corporate officers have raised other serious issues. These unprecedented management betrayals of investor interests have provoked statements that accuse consultants who serve these corporations of opportunism and downright incompetence. Mild statements, compared to more damaging accusations of *"corporate accommodation"* and, as one U.S. Congressman put it, *"prostituting integrity for an outrageous fee"*.

Veteran management consultants are deeply concerned about the motivations and social attitude of many business executives, as well as the degree of integrity of some consulting firms that serve them. These concerns have been around since the early 1940's but at that time, consulting firms were relatively small and preserving a firm's integrity was considerably easier than it is in today's globally positioned consulting firms. Client companies were also smaller before the second world war, and many, like Ford Motor Company, were still controlled by founding entrepreneurs. With the growth and emergence of "Professional Managers", the cultural environment began to change—sometimes for better and often times not.

The all-too-evident dangers from conflicts of interest inherent in permitting a public auditing firm to conduct management consulting services for its audit clients were first raised by Booz Allen & Hamilton, McKinsey and other major management consulting firms in the 1960-1965 period. Maybe these concerns were raised because of the competition of the auditors, but the far greater concern was the possible dilution of integrity within the management consulting profession. These concerns were justified (case-in-point Arthur Anderson), and recent congressional legislation, although twenty years too late, has recognized the extent of the problem.

When and how the seeds of honesty and integrity, in both business and consulting, are best planted, is controversial subject matter for psychologists to ponder. Most agree that the definition, meaning and value of these virtues must be taught at an early stage. Maybe part of the problem is the lack of the course titled *"Honesty, Integrity and Social Responsibility for Managers –101"*, as a requirement in our higher education system.

Unpleasant facts and opinions about consulting ethics are troublesome and of serious concern to the many reputable consulting firms with excellent and unquestioned credentials. These firms, unfairly and unjustifiably, are being tarred with the same brush being applied to the misguided. Wide variations in management performance and observance of high standards of honesty and integrity will always be with us.

Investor trust in the capitalist system, though occasionally shaken, will hold fast. Enron and other scandals have again shaken investor confidence and, disturbingly, recent trends in management performance and responsibility seem to be more negative. Witness the inordinately large executive compensation packages, the greed and the lack of proper corporate governance.

Caught, sometimes in the middle and sometimes on the fringes of the current corporate controversies, consultants will be even more vulnerable to public and investor opinion—and many will have to remould their image. The profession will certainly overcome the current disparagement, but, along the way, some prominent firms will fade, to be replaced by firms with the professional strength and integrity required.

Many companies still view the hiring of a consulting firm as an investment, and when properly chosen, the consultant is an investment that can provide a significant payback. Taking this investment decision requires wide-awake caution by the client, when judging the qualifications and professionalism of the consultant.

In the following chapters we consider how the proper mind-set can be developed and provide you with insights on how various types of consulting organizations will present themselves to you and how they might perform their assignments. But, before going any further, we can immediately disabuse you of the idea that any individual consultant, or livery of consultants, is perfect.

> *Hint Nr. 1*
> *Consultants, even the most prestigious large firms, are not omnipotent and all knowing. They share the market with larger and smaller competitors—some of which are more or less capable, efficient, scrupulous and profitable.*
> *Hint Nr. 2*
> *Consultants are not omniscient. The wisest amongst them know knowledge and innovation has many sources, converges from all directions and does not flow solely from any single individual or from within the walls of any single organization. It follows then, that the consultant should not be relied upon as the sole source of enlightenment. To be of true value, he must constantly seek knowledge absorb it like a sponge and employ it as beneficially as possible, with his best effort, for the interests of his client.*

We have incorporated a well-worn set of rules for self-awareness and it is shown as "Marks of a well-managed company", on the following page. It defines several points for management reflection and indicates areas where consultants can make important contributions.

MARKS OF A WELL-MANAGED COMPANY

*   *   *

A company that nurtures the concept that its vitality and prospects for success depend on the decisiveness and quality of its management talent and on the company commitment which motivates that talent.

A company that understands the extreme value of effective time management and has managers that command time and are not victims of it.

A company that periodically adjusts its organization structure to adapt to new business directions and to eliminate bureaucratic inertia.

A company that subjects itself to a periodic business appraisal which challenges and revitalizes its plan, budget, strategy and objectives.

A company that uses a strategy to bring about change and does not use it only as a tool for sustaining past or current accomplishments.

A company that gives equal priority both to product developments that offer competitive advantages and those that reduce the costs and recycle materials.

A company that looks upon its working capital, less as a means for increasing sales and company size, but more as a means to increase profits.

A company that avoids investment in assets for which it has neither a market, nor an alternative use.

A company that increases its market share by relating to key customers and by also broadening its customer base while also anticipating existing and new technologies and new forms of competition.

Managing the Beast

THE AUTHOR'S PERSPECTIVE

It's anyone's guess how, when or where, someone gave the first advice on how to do something better. There is no doubt that it was long, long before recorded history. Who knows? Could those prehistoric cave and rock drawings have been advice to others about which animals should be avoided and which could be fair game?

Picture this! Once upon a time, long, long ago, someone was pressed to offer advice to someone in desperate need of it. Maybe it was offered to an ancient hunter—some foolish daredevil who, without waiting for the customary combined attack with his hunter companions, had prematurely and foolishly jabbed his spear into the hind quarters of one of those hairy mammoths. Imagine how the furious beast must have been circling to get at his antagonist. The hunter, however foolish, was not a complete idiot and retained enough presence of mind, to refuse to release the spear that separated him from the beast. He flails about at the end of the spear, screaming for help from his friends.

One of the hunters, using grunts and hand signals, advises his terrified companion. His signs are specific. "Don't let go of the spear unless you are sure you can outrun the beast." Now, then—couldn't we say this was very objective and logical advice? Objective and realistic counsel, based on first hand experience in hunting mammoths? Maybe this was how the first qualified, consultant-client relationship was born. We can also safely assume, that in this very first relationship, the consultant had his client's undivided attention.

Consider this case again, for a minute. It would seem that most of the elements of sound consulting were present, qualification by experience, proper problem recognition and analysis, consideration of alternative solutions for the client, good risk evaluation—and a practical and realistic recommendation. We can be generous and assume the hunter outran the beast and validated the consultant's conclusions and advice. Score one for the client—zero for the mammoth. Problem solved.

Today the beasts and the situations confronting the consultant, are different, but the elements of sound advice, give or take the affects of modern technology, have not changed. The client's problem today is to understand his own ability to assess the methods and work quality of the consultant. He must be aware of how the consultant will go about providing the skills required to do the work—and he must know this *before* deciding who might serve him best. A not insignificant task when you consider the size of the consultant population and recognize the inherent variation in consulting quality. In that respect, this book may help make the selection of a *consultant, advisor, expert, or specialist,* somewhat less of a crap-shoot

We all have experiences that influence our approach to managing our lives and our work. I have learned from both successes and failures over a long working career. The learning started with experiences as an hourly paid worker which helped me develop an approach to managing a factory and later managing groups of companies. Nowhere along this path did it appear to me that everything, necessary to be immune to failure had been learned.

*   *   *

There were only a handful of large, American, management consulting firms in the world in the 1950's and 1960's, most of them bound by an agreed set of professional standards. I had the privilege of working in one of the largest firms.

Today, there are thousands of large and very small firms promoting themselves as professional consultants. Significantly larger, is the number of individuals who promote themselves as advisors, specialists or "experts". Clients are therefore confronted with the necessity of determining a consultant's qualifications and professional integrity from a very large field of contenders.

The requirement for entry to a career in consulting has changed, since the 1980's and many senior professionals view this with concern. Qualification for entering the profession today seems to place some inherent, magical value on having earned an MBA. They discount, unexplainably, the value of several years experience working at a full-time job in some industry sector—including work beyond college jobs at a Wendy's, work on an assembly line, or service in the military.

What seems to have been lost on many consulting firms is that there could be more benefit to a client from assigning a consultant who had successfully worked his way up from the shop floor to management, before entering the ranks of a consulting profession.

The work judgement and human relations and leadership skills of a consultant with good work experience in manufacturing, logistics, or sales, should be more valuable in solving a client's problem, than the smart and willing MBA, with none of these qualities. My colleagues and I have found this to be true in serving small and medium size clients in solving operation problems and in providing realistic and practical help for meeting their planning and strategic requirements.

Clients should not be expected to provide on-the-job training to consultants. And, on the other hand, you can't ask a twenty-four year old MBA to have a minimum of ten years of work experience to qualify him for the assignment he is undertaking.

There is an old story that originated in the 1980's—I think it came out of Harvard Law School—and may speak as much to the new breed of consultants as it does to the current style of corporate management.

The Boat Race

A major American automaker and a Japanese automaker were pitted against each other in a rowing race on the Charles River during the 4th of July celebrations. Both crews spent hours in training to reach peak performance levels, and on the 4th of July, the Americans, recognizing the small stature of their competitors, felt they would overwhelm the Japanese crew. Thirty minutes after the starting gun, the Japanese crew had won by a mile.

The American auto maker was very upset by its crew's performance and decided that the reason for the crushing defeat had to be found. They hired a high-profile consulting firm to investigate and to recommend corrective action.

After a year of study and over a million dollars spent on study and analyses, the team of bright, young MBA's had found that the Japanese crew had eight rowers and one steersman. The American crew had two rowers and six people steering.

They concluded there were not enough rowers on the American crew and recommended complete restructuring of the American crew, before the next 4th of July race. The new structure:

Four rowers.
One rowing quality manager at the bow.
One steersman.
Two rowing coaches.

And a new performance review system for the rowers to provide work incentive
The next year the Japanese crew won by two miles.

A meeting was convened at the American company to decide what to do for the
next race. The decision was to lay off the rowers for poor performance and to give
each manager a bonus for discovering the problem.

                   *   *   *

There are, fortunately, more *good*, than *bad* consultants, and the good consulting firms are staffed with highly qualified, professional people who have many years of work experience.

While I draw attention to the chances of making a *bad* choice, this book is largely meant to point out the value to be gained from making the *right* choice of an experienced and qualified consultant. I draw attention to the necessity for prudence and for each client to thoroughly examine the qualifications of the person or firm he contemplates using to assist in making important management decisions.

Experience in corporate management teaches that good consultants are worth the money they charge. While griping about consulting fees, will always be with us. Like everyone else, consultants are in business to make a living. Professional, well-trained and experienced people with high skill levels are in demand, and they are well-paid. But the truth remains that there are some not worth engaging at any price, because the cost of damage control resulting from their work can be very high.

THERE IS NO MAGIC
IN CONSULTING

My firm has had requests for assistance from companies that were submerged in problems and ready to go under for the third time. Their managements were holding out for a miracle. We had the sad duty of telling them that we were not capable of performing the necessary miracle. We have done this, knowing very well, that there would be someone less scrupulous to insist that he could perform the impossible.

Valuing honesty and integrity above all else, a truly professional consultant will always turn down a fee opportunity when he knows the objectives and the salvation of the client are beyond reach. When a consultant is faced with a client situation that he knows is terminal, and the client expects him to provide sudden salvation and is willing to pay any fee for it, the only real miracle would be possession of the magic wand that would do the trick.

What follows takes advantage of long experience in both industry and in consulting, and is intended to provide insight on the proper forms and practices of the consultant. To provide equal insight, they include some of the improprieties that could confront an unwary client. Since a large number of companies, especially small companies, may have little or no experience with consultants, the readers in those companies may be the most likely to benefit.

Our word to the wise company manager is *judiciousness*—be *judicious* in the selection of any outsider you look to for help. When you have a mastadon of a problem, don't be left hanging onto the spear, without good and logical advice at hand.

CHAPTER ONE

GETTING ORIENTED

Company managers have frequently hired consultants to assist in problem solving, or to provide temporary reinforcement for their planning, strategy, marketing, manufacturing or engineering needs. There are a few who have never hired a consultant, and some managers, more than likely, never will. But this leaves a significant number inclined to approach an outside source for assistance of some kind.

There aren't many statistics on this seventy-odd year old profession and, even though the United States has the highest population of business card-carrying consultants, only about twenty-five percent of American and European companies have ever hired one. *(The reader should exclude auditing, accounting and tax services, which do not fall within the framework of management consulting as it is addressed in this book.)*

A few large auditing and accounting firms such as Price Waterhouse Cooper or Deloite Touche, provide strategic and operations management consulting services. This practice of one firm providing both these services to the same client has been controversial for many years. Established management consulting firms have long made the strong argument that this practice raises opportunity for conflict of interest and exposes the client to counsel of doubtful integrity.

Considering the author's foregoing, built-in bias, the reader is advised that this book addresses consulting as—operations and general *management consulting* and, within the frame of this narrower definition, can be found the majority of professional consulting services.

THE MORE COMMON SERVICES PROVIDED BY MANAGEMENT CONSULTANTS

- Business, product, market planning and strategy, budgetary planning and control and organization development

- Market research, competitive strategies and technology assessment

- Organization planning, organization structure and job definition, human resources selection, training and development

- Operations analyses, cost reduction, productivity improvement, including manufacturing systems, processes, controls research in materials, processes and product technology

THE CLIENT'S FIRST STEP IS SELF-ORIENTATION, BEFORE DECIDING TO LOOK FOR OUTSIDE ASSISTANCE

Before inviting an external service to assist in any of the areas shown above, management should have identified and thoroughly examined the company's needs and carefully specified the need for outside assistance. By so doing, there is a better chance of achieving results that provide a positive impact on the company. In other words:

1. Be sure you have identified and understood your problem.
2. Be able to describe it succinctly to the consultant.
3. Have a reasonable, achievable and quantified objective for the consultant to achieve by the end of his assignment—the "deliverables".
4. Be sure that the consultant has the acceptance of top management and that he will be provided the necessary communications and logistics support for him to carry out his assignment quickly and effectively.

Develop the attitude, at all levels of your company, that the use of outside assistance is only temporary—a *"one-off"* situation—and should be looked upon as an investment that will provide management with another decision tool to help achieve company goals. Management must immediately defuse any suspicion of intended, negative impact on the company organization from the consultant's assignment. Management must foster understanding among managers and employees that the consultant is being engaged as another asset to increase efficiency and provide competitive and profit benefits for the company.

THE CONSULTANT CAN BE A DISCRETE INTERFACE BETWEEN TOP MANAGEMENT, FUNCTIONAL STAFFS, OUTSIDE INFORMATION SOURCES AND OTHER COMPANIES, AGENCIES AND INSTITUTIONS.

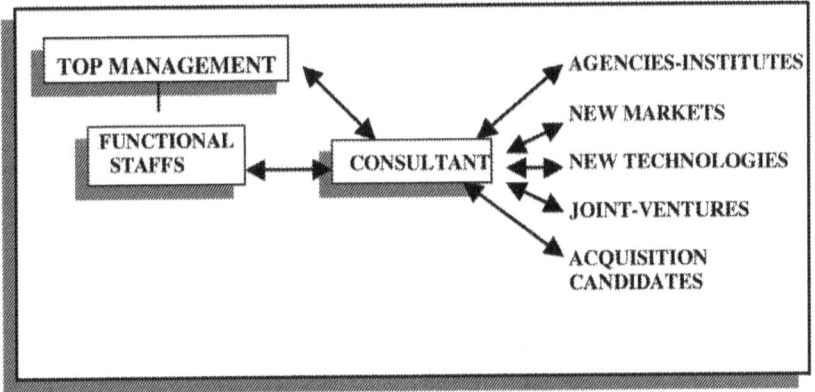

KNOW WHERE TO LOOK FOR OUTSIDE ASSISTANCE

Finding the assistance that is best for your specific need is no simple task. Although consultants are as numerous as fleas on a junk- yard hound, there are no directories that grade their performance or quality. However, there are directories that list various types of consulting services and provide contact information and a short profile of the firm, or individual. One example of several industry specific directories is one published by the Society of Automotive Engineers (SAE), listing automotive industry consultants.

So, how do you locate the consultant that can best serve you?

If you don't mind letting it be known that you are looking for help, start by canvassing companies you know have used consultants. You can surf the internet. Almost any established, professional firm of good repute has developed a website to inform potential clients of its services and many are industry sector specific. Check with your purchasing department, because consultants *come-a-knocking* quite often, and they may have left information in your purchasing manager's service sources file.

About sixty percent of consulting assignments are undertaken because the client was referred by someone who has had previous dealings with the consultant. This means that once you have located a consultant that looks like he may be right for you, have him provide you with professional references from clients for whom he has carried out similar assignments in the past. Even with apparently good references, it is necessary to do your own thorough investigation of the consultant. It is equally necessary to be able to assess the information he provides in a face-to-face interview, or in presentations of his services. Even that old junk-yard hound has to scratch around until he feels comfortable.

CHAPTER TWO

WHAT YOU SHOULD EXPECT FROM THE CONSULTANT

All of us are fallible, regardless of our education, our experience, skills, or any other of our special endowments. None of us can stand alone as examples of perfection. It is reasonable, therefore, that any client must anticipate less than 100% in the results of any consulting assignment. The key to limiting imperfection, therefore, is be judicious in selecting the person, or firm you use and to be equally judicious in how you evaluate, validate and use the consultant's advice.

Recognize that the quality of service provided in any work assignment seldom has anything to do with the size of the consulting organization—but has everything to do with experience, knowledge and skill of the individuals assigned to carry out the work. Insist that any team assigned by the consulting firm be highly skilled, properly qualified, experienced and fully backed by the firm's past assignment experience in the particular problem area where you are seeking assistance. Be aware that the experience and makeup of the consulting team can vary widely and can positively or adversely affect the assignment you give them. More on this subject later.

Once you have provided the consultant with clear assignment objectives, you should expect him to provide a written proposal that defines his understanding of the problem, the methodology he will employ in solving it, the time required and the fee and expenses estimate to complete the work. The proposal is a key element and serves as an offer which is agreed in writing by the client as a form of acceptance. This is a critical and mandatory step in the formalities of dealing with a consultant. Many misunderstandings between client and consultant stem from ambiguous terms of a proposal, or where nothing more than a verbal proposal was offered and agreed. The difficulty usually comes when the work is completed and both parties interpret the objectives and the "deliverables" differently.

The consultant should be expected to apply his best efforts and skills in accomplishing the assignment given him. He is obligated to providing practical and realistic solutions, developed from facts he has gathered and verified on which he has based logical assumptions and recommendations. You should expect him to be immune to any influence pressed on him by your company's internal politics, biases, or by internal promotion of personal agendas. Stated another way, you should expect the consultant to resist undue influences that would prostitute his efforts, or urge him to support pre-conceived and unfounded conclusions that are meant to serve unwarranted, special interests within your organization.

You must expect honesty, integrity and discretion to rule every element of the consultant's work activities and the final counsel he provides.

A REPUTABLE CONSULTANT WILL DECLINE TO ACCEPT SOME ASSIGNMENTS

A reputable consultant will not accept assignments for work he feels it is not qualified to carry out. He will be reluctant to take on an assignment, knowing that success, or benefits to the client, would at best be minimal. The responsible consultant understands that integrity should not be compromised for the sake of an easy fee.

Not all consultants take this stand, however, and there are firms who will undertake any assignment for a fee, knowing that the outcome will be of no value to the client. Consulting firms that fall in this category are, too frequently, those who have highly paid "business developers", who derive their income and promotions mainly from their ability to develop and close sales of assignments.

A reputable consultant will never compromise his findings to suit the wishes of the client. He will provide accurate data and objectiveness, even if it goes against the client's expectations.

Consultants have lost follow-on assignments from clients, after they provided conclusions that contradicted, or undermined the position taken by client management. You, the client, should expect your consultant to have the courage and integrity to show you that you are wrong, but he must be able to do so without incurring your animosity. You should also expect him to be astute and recommend logical, reasonable and realistic action alternatives along with each problem solution.

EXPECT CONTINUITY OF SERVICE

The consultant should be available for future follow-up discussions in the event that any new management members need to be oriented, or want to review the work the consultant did prior to their arrival.

The consulting profession has a high rate of staff turnover, mainly because client companies often recruit management from the consultant's ranks. You should expect, and receive, assurances that the work done for you will be backed by the security of organizational continuity. Simply stated, you expect the consulting firm to be around for the long-term, and have the means to resurrect the detail and rationale used for the work it has performed. If the key consultant who carried out the assignment is run over by a truck, there should be someone else in the firm who can carry the ball with equal, or more competence.

EXPECT THE CONSULTANT TO CONTROL FEE COSTS

Clients all too often will want to change the work content of the assignment, which affects the fee and expenses. Both the client and the consultant should agree, in writing, changes in the assignment and the change agreement should specify any increase or decrease in the overall fee structure of the assignment.

Expect the consultant to stay within the agreed fee, or fee-range, that was established in the proposal agreement, including any fee increase or decrease resulting from agreed changes in the ongoing work content. Periodic progress reports, including status of fee charges, should be expected from the consultant to avoid any accumulation of unsettled problems in the assignment.

Reputable firms will charge only for time and expenses actually incurred during the assignment. This provides cost benefit to the client when work is completed in less than the allotted time budget agreed in the initial assignment proposal.

Expenses can be heavy in assignments that require significant travel. You should agree, therefore, on the class of travel and category of living accommodation to be used by the consulting team and expect them to observe these limitations.

Keep in mind that when you build a relationship with a good, professional consultant, he too desires to maintain good relations with his clients as a dependable source of new assignments each year. It is in both his and the client's best interests when he performs his task well. Generally, you should be optimistic that his performance will meet your requirements, and if you have been *judicious* in your selection, that should be the case.

CHAPTER THREE

Overload

SITUATIONS THAT FREQUENTLY CALL FOR THE USE OF A CONSULTANT

Financial and operating problems are not the only conditions prompting companies to reach for outside assistance. Experience has shown that most consulting assignments come from clients that are in good financial condition, but need independent counseling in business strategy, marketing and in coping with new technologies and company development. Most assignments in the operating systems and control areas come about from overload of the client's permanent staff where temporary assistance from the outside is needed.

Pointing to experience again, we can categorize the most frequent situations that call for assistance from a consultant

- Clients needing assistance in business planning and strategy development
- Clients needing an evaluation of their own and other company (usually competitors), operations
- Clients in need of assistance in marketing research, planning and management and in human relations and management development
- Clients in need of operational cost and functional improvement

CLIENTS WITH BUSINESS PLANNING AND STRATEGIC DEVELOPMENT NEEDS

During the past two decades, many companies have been inspired or forced by competition to sail into unfamiliar waters in search of new markets, new products, growth, greater profitability, a more satisfactory return on shareholder investment and an increase in shareholder value. Insufficient preparation for this voyage has placed investments in jeopardy for some, while others found that they should have solved problems in their core business, rather than attempting to camouflage them through diversification via acquisition of other companies.

What types of companies do we find needing assistance in these areas? Here are a few examples from our client case records.

- Companies with operations that are expanding too fast
- Young companies entering into fast moving markets
- Companies that have diversified too fast from the core business
- Companies needing re-organization after a merger or acquisition
- Static companies with slow growth and poor financial performance
- Companies losing market position and needing new products and markets
- Companies entering high technology markets from a low technology base

Consultants monitor companies in any of the situations shown above and are most always in the front line, selling the idea that there is a need for an objective and experienced assessment of the company's needs, and for the determination of alternatives for satisfying those needs.

CLIENTS IN NEED OF AN EVALUATION OF THEIR OWN OR OTHER COMPANIES

We have quite often found that closely held companies have only vague ideas of what their business is worth on the acquisition (M&A) market. Accounting firms and banks often having little or no special knowledge of the industry or the business niche, have a tendency to formularize value, rather than assess value in terms of market share, competitive strength, product technology, or product and company image. Employing an outside, industry specialist has proven to be beneficial to shareholders in the company situations noted below.

- Owners wishing to sell their company
- Investment groups contemplating share purchases
- Banks making large loans
- Companies acquiring or divesting companies
- Joint-Venture participants wanting an independent evaluation of each other's capability to perform his part of the venture

CLIENTS NEEDING ASSISTANCE IN MARKET PLANNING, STRATEGY AND MANAGEMENT

Client companies often reach out for foreign markets as a way to accelerate company growth and have found that international consulting firms can be a valuable resource for market research and analyses and for providing insights in the location of new products for both old and new markets.

- Companies searching for new markets for new products, or processes
- Companies looking for new markets for traditional products or processes
- Companies looking for new products for current markets

One important aspect in selecting a consultant in the marketing area is to be sure the individual or team has a thorough knowledge of the geographic market, the competitors, and the product technology involved. It is sometimes difficult to find these three qualifications when an assignment is world wide in scope.

CLIENTS IN NEED OF OPERATIONS IMPROVEMENT

Operations analyses are, in many cases, required as a first step to improving functional efficiency and making cost improvements. A thorough analysis, sometimes called a "diagnostic study" determines the root problems and from there, a comprehensive program for improvements implementation or turn around plan can be developed.

Even in the most technical and highly automated operations, humans are the implementers who will bring success or failure, and must be factored in as the key element in any success equation. In no segment of industry has the human element been eliminated. Where there are people involved, operations analyses and improvement programs demand that the consultant be well versed in anticipating the impact from introducing changes that affect managers and workers. It is equally important that the client management be fully in support of any operational changes that they have agreed should be implemented.

The benefits from using an experienced consultant who has been exposed to similar problems in a number of different companies can be great and can bring innovations that might not have been identified by the company, on its own. Some of the common situations where consultants are used are shown below.

- Clients with materials and/or other assets control problems
- Clients with cost control and/or cost reduction needs
- Clients with multiple plant operations needing facilities rationalization to reduce transport, inventories, capital and labor costs
- Clients selecting new plant locations and involved in "greenfield" start-ups where they are short of project management.
- Clients with manufacturing process, process qualification and quality management problems

The foregoing are only a few of the common situations calling for use of a consultant. Often there is a difference of opinion between the various functional heads of a company relative to such subjects as product viability, product strategy, market strategy, the life cycle of products during rapid changes in product technology, and many other issues. In these situations top management may want an independent, outside evaluation of the issues, to either confirm, or modify the client's thinking. In these cases, a good, qualified consultant can present facts uninhibited by influences from conflicting agendas within the client organization. With the increasing trend to downsize (get lean), throughout industry, demand for short-term specialists is increasing in North America, Europe and many other regions of the world. As this trend increases, it is necessary that the client be very diligent in selecting the most qualified assistance available. The following case illustrates the "fixing" sometimes required after a client has acted on unqualified advice.

Case of the traction device

In the 1980's, a large machinery builder in America was contemplating the purchase of the patent rights to a mechanical traction device for use in automotive applications. The engineering head was enthusiastic about the new technology, but the heads of marketing and finance were very skeptical. The Chairman of the company asked my firm to evaluate the patented device and assess its marketing potential in automotive vehicles and we agreed to do so. As automotive specialists, we determined the device to have good potential as a traction control feature for light military vehicles as a first market target and recommended the purchase of the patent rights.

The client did development work and succeeded in having it applied in a military vehicle. Later, acting on the advice of another consulting firm, the device was put into production in one of the company's European machine tool plants not experienced in high volume series production. The consultant recommended installation of highly sophisticated and automated transfer lines linking materials storage and improperly qualified production machinery. The results were serious production, quality and customer problems. Once again we were asked to put things right and sent in a team to separate the traction device from the machine tool operation. The team installed materials management, tool and quality control, solved some design weaknesses reduced manufacturing automation and subcontracted foundry and heat treat work, resulting in a 40% manufacturing cost reduction.

We have since carried out numerous operations and strategic assignments for this client.

CHAPTER FOUR

PREPARING FOR THE CONSULTANT

A GOOD CONSULTANT MAY LIVE WITH YOUR ORGANIZATION FOR ONLY A SHORT TIME, BUT HIS CONTRIBUTIONS CAN LEAVE LASTING BENEFITS

Managers can lose sight of the fact that the success of an assignment carried out by a consultant can only be a success for the client. In other words, an objective agreed by the client and reached by the consultant constitutes success.

If you have chosen a reputable consulting firm, the firm cannot afford or tolerate sub-standard or incomplete work to be presented. The firm will be conscientious enough, and bound close enough to the interests of its client, that the firm will make an effort to give more than 100% of what was contracted to be provided. Doesn't it seem obvious that all client managers should be enthusiastic in their support of and co-operation with the consultant? How nice that would be, if such were the case in each assignment.

Experience over many years, on many assignments in hundreds of companies, has taught that most failures in the use of qualified consultants are due to client failure to prepare for the consultant for one or more of the following reasons.

- Failure to clearly define the client's objectives and describe the work he wants the consultant to provide. This should be defined as provision of:
  Concept development only
  Concept and design of systems or operations
  Design and installation of systems
  Diagnose problems, identify solutions and implement them
  Diagnose operations, provide action plans and manage the turn-around implementation

- Failure of client management to introduce the consultant and describe his role and provide for co-operation within the client organization
- Client doubt in the solutions recommended by the consultant
- Too little supervision of the consulting team by the consulting firm's management and inadequate dialogue with and progress reporting to the client
- Lack of client disclosure of data and conditions relevant to the work of the consultant
- Failure of the consultant to provide realistic solutions to client problems, or failure to provide help in implementing solutions

Preparing for the logistic support of a team of consultants who will be working within the client facilities is important and should be appropriate to the complexity, sensitivity and confidentiality of the assignment. When client personnel have open access to the consultant's unsecured work area it can present "grapevine" distortions.

DO NOT EXPECT THE CONSULTANT
TO BE EITHER A "STAR", OR A "SUIT".

The experienced and successful consultant is neither a "*Suit*" nor is he a "*Star*"—he is a student of human nature, a collector of information, and an objective analyst with no preconceived conclusions. The experienced   professional is a good listener, circumspect and discrete. His objective is to make the client shine—not to focus undue attention on himself—and to leave the client with values that are multiples of the fees he has been paid.

Be prepared for the fact that the senior general management consultant assigned to head up your assignment may be qualified and experienced to undertake any management position in your company, and do it well—in other words, be ready to treat him as your equal until he proves to be less. If the consultant is all that he is expected to be, you will feel comfortable in your relationship with him.

There will also be occasions to welcome a professional consultant who is a specialist in a narrower discipline or function, but he may be no less valuable to you than the generalist described above.

Preparing well for the arrival of the consultant sets the stage for successful completion of an assignment, and for minimum repercussions in the middle management and labor force.

CHAPTER FIVE

HAVE THE CONSULTANT COMMIT TO A DETAILED PROPOSAL

The formal proposal identifies the objectives, work elements, time schedule and cost agreed by both consultant and client.

Entering into an assignment without a formal and detailed proposal and acceptance is an invitation to revel in confusion, disagreement and usually winds up in "I said, you said" recriminations. This is all too often the case when inexperienced consultants and the managers of small companies use verbal and short memoranda as the basis for entering into consulting projects. When longer-term assignments are involved, these types of relationships result in misinterpretations of intent, objectives, or results (deliverables), expected. There can also be difficulties in "passing the torch", on the assignment when changes in either consultant or client personnel take place.

BEWARE OF "BAIT AND SWITCH"

Usually a proposal is prepared and presented by a senior member of the consulting firm; someone whose major activity is business development in the consulting area involved in the proposal. He will appear in dignified uniform in response to your request for a preliminary meeting to discuss your needs. He may also arrive in response to written specifications which you have sent his firm. You will, more than likely, recognize him as a top rank specialist in the subject of discussion and he will do his best to infer that he will prepare the proposal and be personally responsible for the management of your project. And sometimes this may actually be the case. But, more often than not, you will see little or nothing of him as a member of the consulting team when the work takes place. He may or may not be on hand when the final report is presented. This man is the *"Bait"* with which to hook you and make the sale.

A variation on this approach is to have another consultant, a highly qualified and experienced specialist in the subject problem area, accompany the business development specialist. This is a double barrel approach to "*baiting*" the client. In this case, as well, you may find that this specialist has little involvement in actually carrying out any of the project work. Sometimes the proposal states that the specialist (*the support bait*), will be responsible only for vetting the quality of the work of the team. And he may appear, in the back row, to add credence to the findings when the audio-visual summary presentation of the report is made. Unless you have arranged differently, the work will be carried out by a team of consultants and technicians that may be good, but of lesser substance than the "*bait man*".

Again, it would be wise for the client to have the actual time involvement of this specialist specified in the proposal, describing what his real input responsibilities are to be and providing for periodic status reports from him.

The "*switch*" part is evident to you when the consulting work team arrives and you find that the "*bait*" is not with them. Instead, you have a group of relatively junior consultants on your doorstep. This misleading practice can be avoided by assuring that all team members are identified and qualified in the proposal, and that a profile is provided for each.

"Bait and switch" is often encountered in projects involving large consulting teams, where the project fee is sizeable, or where the team is smaller, but the duration of the project is longer than 12 months. These are coveted assignments for large consulting firms which employ managers or partners whose main function is business development.

"*Bait and switch*" is not inferred when a significant amount of the day-to-day assignment work is carried out by one or more of the consultants who developed and presented the proposal to the client. Although this is the respectable manner in which most consulting jobs are sold and carried out, there is still need to be aware of the exceptions.

A WELL WRITTEN PROPOSAL AVOIDS LATER PROBLEMS

Depending on the nature and complexity of the client's problem, or his service requirement, the consultant can select one or two paths in making a proposal and carrying out the assignment.

If the assignment is one with which the consultant has much experience and the nature of the problem is clear, he might adopt the following approach:

- He will make a preliminary visit to get the client's input on the sophistication level and extent of the work required.
- He will present a written proposal describing his understanding of the objectives, the methodology to be used and the cost.
- When the proposal is agreed, he will carry out the work.
- He will present conclusions and recommendations for discussion, prior to publishing the final report.
- He will prepare and make a summary presentation of the report and his recommendations to the client management.

When the assignment involves a more complex and not clearly defined problem the consultant may want to take a two-stage approach:

- He will make a preliminary visit to get client inputs and to review the company operations.
- He will provide a proposal to carry out a short study to define the problem more clearly.
- He will conduct the study and report his findings and present a detail proposal for the main body of the assignment to be agreed.
- He will carry out the main body of the work.
- He will present conclusions and recommendations for implementing the solutions to the client management, prior to writing his final report.
- He will present the final report, in summary, with his recommendations and with a plan for implementation.

In both approaches, a detailed proposal is presented to the client for his agreement on the consultant's understanding of the objectives and:

- How he will go about conducting the work,
- What the key elements of the report will include,
- Who will be assigned to do the work,
- The consultant's qualifications for conducting the assignment,
- The time it will take to complete the work,
- Fee and expense costs

A properly drawn proposal can avoid misinterpretations of objectives and expected elements of the final report and the assignment will follow the work logic depicted in the chart shown below.

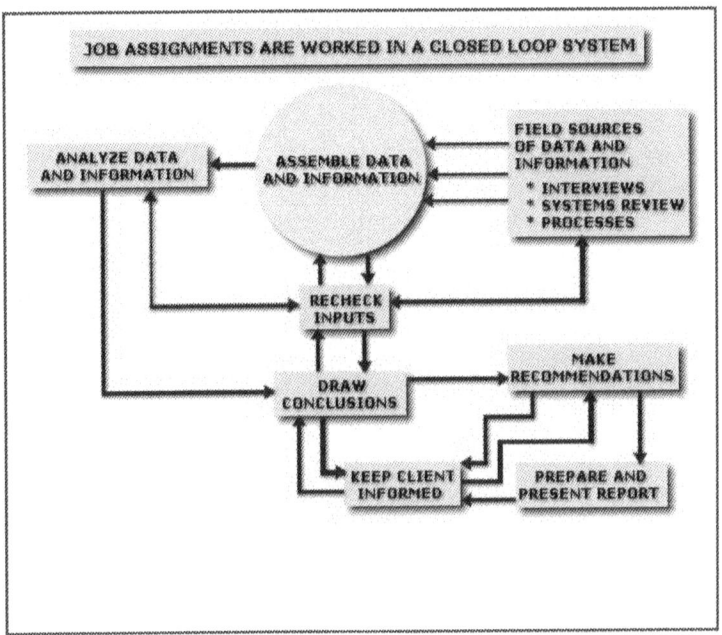

MULTI-CLIENT PROPOSALS

Not all proposals in recent years have been for single client assignments. Studies sponsored by groups of companies have emerged as an economic way of obtaining valuable information on new technology developments and applications, well within the reach of small and medium size company budgets.

Multi-client studies are different in that the consultant provides the same proposal to a number of companies involved with, or having interest in, a specific product, technology, or market. These studies are usually world wide in scope, take 5 to 8 months to complete and are expensive to conduct. The advantage to the individual sponsors in sharing the information of the study is, quite reasonably, the distribution of the study cost among the sponsors. By this tactic, a study with a $200,000 budget can be made available to each of 10 sponsors for one tenth of the overall study cost. The number of sponsors necessary to cover the study cost must be committed before the study work begins.

The sponsor must be assured that the product of a multi-client study is specified in detail in the proposal and that the information resulting has use for future planning and strategy development. Detailed tomes of statistics and history without insights and projections that reach out at least 10 years are of suspect value. The sponsor should be aware that application projections for new technologies and growth projections for new and untested markets are, many times, overly optimistic when made by consultants who have only a shallow knowledge of the subject, and do not have perspective on competing and emerging technologies.

Most multi-client studies are designed for top management as tools for planning and strategy development, and usually have to do with emerging technologies, and their viability in various markets. They can be a serious and economic addition to the intelligence of the sponsoring company.

CHAPTER SIX

STAFFING THE ASSIGNMENT

Your responsibility as the client is to see that the consulting assignment is properly staffed and properly supervised by an officer or partner of the consulting firm. This responsibility is made easier if you have had the consulting firm identify and qualify each consultant in the initial proposal.

Most consulting firms with 20 or more professionals have a mix of senior and junior consultants and research technicians. The proportions of this mix applied to your assignment is very important and during the proposal stage you should expect, at the very least, a ratio of 4 senior consultants to every 10 employees on the consulting firm's payroll.

A senior consultant is defined here as a professional with at least 10 years of management experience in industry. If the team assigned to your company numbers 5 consultants, you should expect that at least 2 will be senior professionals.

The level of skills used in "selling a consulting job", as we have seen, can be higher than the skill levels applied in carrying out the work assignment. Guard against surprises by seeing curriculum vitae for each consultant the firm intends to put on your job. You should also insist on a staffing plan when the assignment is a long one and team members are to be rotated in and out of the assignment for different phases of the work. Be sure that you will have benefit of senior level consultants in proper proportion to the total man-days of the project.

As an illustration of how staffing proposals for the same client assignment from three different consulting firms (A, B and C), can vary, we have shown the fee cost and man-day mix in a typical market research assignment. In the illustration firms A and B provide a good mix of supervision and skills, while firm C provides a minimum of supervision and skills. The lower level of supervision and heavy use of junior consultants in "C", permits a much lower fee cost, but also permits a much higher opportunity for less than optimal results.

Staffing		"A"	"B"	"C"
Officer	$1500/day	4 days = $6000	4 days = $6000	2 days = $3000
Sr. Consultant	$1000/day	6 days = $6000	16 days = $16000	
Consultant	$800/day	15 days = $12000		11 days = $8800
Jr. Consultant	$400/day	13 days = $5200	17 days = $6800	24 days = $9600
Totals		38 days = $29,200	37 days = $28800	37 days = $21400

A TYPICAL MARKET RESEARCH ASSIGNMENT FOR A SMALL COMPANY CAN VARY IN CONSULTING FEE COST, DEPENDING ON THE STAFFING OF THE ASSIGNMENT

Firm A ➡ Good mix of supervision and skill levels

Firm B ➡ High level of supervision and skills applied

Firm C ➡ Minimal supervision and skills mix applied

If you were to make a choice from the above illustration, it would be up to you to determine whether, or not, the consultant and junior consultant to be used by firm "C", were of high caliber and experienced enough to carry out the work for you. You might be fortunate and find that, in this exceptional case, these represent excellent staffing choices—or you may not.

Look closely at the mix of talent and experience of the consulting team. A predominance of junior consultant time may open the door to undue influence on the project work conclusions from client company managers. Client influence might be weighed differently by more senior consultants and would, more likely, be resisted.

It is the individual consultants assigned to the job who determine the quality of your project work. Whether your consulting team is part of a small firm, or part of a glitter-image consultancy with a high public relations budget, the product of the team will reflect its own collective merits and professionality. You should also consider that the proposal with the lowest fee may indicate a lower level of professional skills, and when applied to your project, may not always produce satisfactory results.

THE CONSULTANT MUST UNDERSTAND YOUR TECHNOLOGY

The technology explosion taking place in many industry sectors, such as automotive, telecom, electronics, pharmaceuticals, demands that the consultant dealing with product and market strategy be acutely aware of emerging innovations and product developments, as well as the changes in economics and consumer demands taking place in your product area. The level of this awareness will affect any attempt at market forecasts and a low level of awareness of emerging technologies may foster overly optimistic market projections over a 5-10 year period.

Two cases of overly optimistic forecasts for technologies in the automotive industry, for example, involved active suspension and four wheel steering. The faulty forecasting in both cases were the result of focusing on the new technology and neglecting the economics and alternative technology choices for the consumer. A properly qualified consulting team would have arrived at a far less optimistic forcast for the application of these two technologies.

BIGGER IS NOT ALWAYS BETTER

A major selling point for the very large consultancies is their ability to put together large consulting teams for very large projects. Some projects may require that as many as 30 to 50 consultants be assigned to work many locations in parallel. Although a smaller firm may be equally or more highly qualified and have international operations, the size factor gives the larger firm the manpower edge in carrying out major projects for clients such as large government agencies, or other public or private organizations especially when it involves work in many wide-spread domestic and foreign locations.

Operating from many locations also gives the larger consulting firms an important advantage in the scope of business development activity and in the ability to provide customer service proximity. The large firm, on the down side, may be at a disadvantage when headquarters requires a tight rein on service quality at every location.

First hand experience has taught that it is easier to manage the quality of service, the objectiveness, the spirit and morale of staff colleagues in a consulting firm with 50 to 100 professionals, than it is to manage these things in a firm with 2000 professionals. In the larger firm, the inherent quality dispersion is usually much wider than it is in the smaller firm. It is also much easier for the top management in your company to maintain a close relationship with the top management of the smaller consulting firm. You will find it more difficult to maintain the same relationship with a large firm handling hundreds of demanding clients.

Every client relationship is critical to the smaller firms and all are usually carefully managed. The perspective of the top management of the very large consulting firm might be more related to numbers, and the gain or loss of a single client may be less critical than it would be to the smaller firm. You could, of course, expect the larger firm to maintain a close relationship with your top management if you are a very major and consistant fee provider.

The smaller consulting firm usually has an advantage in not being burdened by the cost of maintaining large offices at prestigious addresses. The computer, internet and e-mail have permitted the downsizing of support locations and in most of these smaller firms, the consultant works from a home office, or at client premises, and only occasionally at the regional office. The smaller firm is flexible in adjusting its logistics to meet client demands, and in many cases they have founded associations with a number of free-lance specialists for supporting project teams on client assignments. We define a "smaller" consulting firm as one with 20 to 30 permanent professional staff and 10 to 20 "on-call", free lance specialists that work on a project-to-project basis. A firm working in a narrow, highly specialized area, on the other hand, might require only a handful of consultants and technicians.

You might qualify the size factor in this way. Think of it in terms of the discerning executive who elects to enjoy the superb meals and personal attention provided by a small, gourmet restaurant. His service expectations are higher than that of the executive who takes his meals at the factory cafeteria. Sometimes smaller can be better. The following case illustrates a situation where the approach of a smaller firm differed greatly from that of a large consulting firm, mainly because of its specific skills in the client's problem area.

Case of the "musical chairs game" in regional warehouses

One of the larger, international consulting firms was called into a major supplier of engine components to determine why the company's shipping and transport costs were three times that of its competitors. The firm arrived with a team of six consultants to analyze the order processing, shipping and receiving activities of the main plant and each of the 16 regional warehouses. After three months, the resulting report recommended that the company lease a fleet of its own trucks and cancel its contracts with commercial trucking companies, creating a cost saving of about $300,000 per year. The client managing director read the report and decided he should call in a consultant he had used in a previous company.

Two members of the smaller firm arrived, read the report and started their own investigation. After two weeks, the logistics and inventory consultants reported that the problem was due to improper inventory management and lack of inventory activity reporting between the factory and the regional warehouses. The high costs were not due to movement of stocks to customers, but was due to the transfer of inventory from warehouse to warehouse, to cover stock shortages. This was caused by failure to do seasonal balancing of stocks, in anticipation of peak demand periods—periods that varied from warehouse to warehouse. This resulted in a constant game of musical chairs as the excess items were transferred to shortage locations. As a consequence, about one third of the total field inventory was being moved a minimum of six times per year, to cover unnecessary shortages at each warehouse location.

One consultant was left behind, for two weeks, to work with the EDP department and install new A,B,C, inventory rules and establish daily computer reporting of item-by-item activity to control warehouse stocking shipments that would match seasonal requirements coverage. The result was an overall increase in "first pick" to 86% on filled order shipments to customers, a fifty percent reduction in shipping and transport costs and a twenty percent reduction in overall warehouse inventories. The annualized cost savings from transport and inventory reduction was confirmed by client audit at about $1,200,000.

The cost of the work by the larger firm—$165,000

The cost of the smaller firm—$55,000

CHAPTER SEVEN

CONSULTING FEE RATES—OUCH!

You should not be surprised to learn that fees for consultants range from as little as $600, to as much as $5,000 per man-day, depending on the degree of expertise required, and the technology or functional discipline involved. An expert in computer chip processing, for example, could demand up to $500 per hour for his time, whereas a logistics consultant might demand $100 per hour. A senior general management consultant specializing in strategy development, or company restructuring and crisis management, can demand $2,500 per day, plus a success bonus.

HOW DAILY FEES ARE DETERMINED

The fee rate for a senior consultant will vary, depending on the size of the firm and its overhead structure. The very large firms, such as McKinsey, Booz Allen & Hamilton, Boston Group, and Bain, have high overhead structure costs that must be included in the fee structure. Smaller firms have lower burdens reflected in their daily rates.

The established consulting firm usually has a set fee for each consultant on its professional staff. These individual fees vary according to the special knowledge, skill and experience of the consultant, and will vary also according to his rank in the firm. However, there is no fixed rule for setting fee rates throughout the consulting service sector.

Consulting firms, in general, expect to keep an individual consultant on paid assignment work for 180 billable days each year, out of an average 210 working days each year. The 180 days of fee work must cover the individual consultant's full annual compensation, plus a contribution to overhead, business development cost and an add-on for a reasonable contribution to profit.

Bonus contributions to profit appear when the consultant is able to bill more than 180 fee days in the year. Since a billing week represents a time charge of 40 hours, a work week with extra billable hours, including Saturday, reduces the number of calendar days required to reach the 180 fee billing days. These billing days above 180 go almost entirely to the firm's bottom line. Long term projects often create opportunities to compress the project time plan and provide more profit from an individual consultant's activities during the year.

A multiplier is applied to the full compensation recovery to arrive at a daily fee billing rate. The daily, full compensation rate is calculated by dividing the consultant's annual compensation by 180—the number of fee days in which his, or her, compensation has to be recovered. The resulting daily fee rate for compensation recovery is then multiplied from 2 to 4 times, or more, to arrive at the total daily fee rate charged to the client. The fee multiplier used depends upon the size and type of consulting firm. An example of the multiplier, related to the firm size is shown below.

Multiplier	Size of Firm	Consultants
2	Small firm,	10-20 professionals
2.5	Specialized firm,	20-50 "
3	Medium firm	50-100 "
4+	Large firm	250+ "

A consultant with a yearly compensation of, say, $60,000, would have a base recovery fee of:

$$\frac{\$60,000}{180} = \$333 \text{ per day}$$

Therefore, the total fee billing rate for each firm size above would be:

	Multiplier	Daily Billing Rate
Small firm	2	$666
Specialized firm	2.5	$832
Medium firm	3	$999
Large firm	4	$1332

The illustration above is an indication of the much higher billing rates that can be charged for partners or managers in some firms. A partner in a larger firm, for example, can have a $3,000 daily billing rate.

So, when the consulting firm knocks on your door and displays his wares, be judicious—and don't wind up paying more for the frosting than for the cake.

Competition is a strong, mitigating influence on determining fee charges in a proposal and since the late 1990's both large and small consulting firms have had to adopt a *"what the market (client), will bear"* strategy in an increasingly more difficult and competitive business development environment. Frankly, a large corporate client will usually bear a higher fee rate than will small and medium size companies, even in times of economic downturn. Additionally, daily fees charged on a long-term assignment will tend to be lower than fees for a short-term job. This fee difference is generally justified by the lower business development cost per fee day for a long-term project, than for a short-term assignment.

If you draw the conclusion that consulting fees are somewhat negotiable depending on the industry, the client's size, the economic environment and the total number of man-days involved, then you would be correct. You should definitely bear this in mind during negotiations with the consultant.

DON'T LET THE CONSULTANT FIRM'S PAID PUBLIC RELATIONS AND ADVERTISING BE THE SOLE BASIS FOR THEIR SERVICE QUALIFICATIONS

The large consulting firms have sizeable budgets for PR promotion, glossy advertisements, television advertisement and exposure from sports sponsorship. These tools are, without question, important for image and business development, but do not necessarily provide an accurate picture of the firm's qualifications and only infer their ability to carry out your service needs.

When major assignments, such as *"core business"* analyses and *corporate restructuring* studies are required, they most often involve agreement at the board level before proceeding. The tendency is for the board members to favor high-profile consulting firms over smaller and equally or better qualified firms. This is, more-or-less, the *"costs be damned"* rationale.

The most frequently stated reason for this choice, in my experience, is that the shareholders will feel more comfortable with a "big" name, when major and costly changes are dictated by the outcome of these types of assignments. In other words, they do not want the shareholders to say "who?" when the consultant firm is announced—they want it to be quickly recognized by everyone.

A number of smaller consulting firms also have someone aboard who spends full time building a company PR image. Large and small firms benefit from quotes appearing in business and financial magazines and journals, but the smaller firms rarely advertise on a large scale. Do not rely on the "PR" image of either the large or smaller firm as the qualification for carrying out an assignment for you. Go through all the steps mentioned earlier and be judicious in your evaluation and in your selection.

AUDIT THE FEE CHARGES

In the case of assignments that run for many months, there is always an arrangement for the consultant to bill fees and expenses on a monthly basis. When a large consulting team of 10 or more is charging time each month, the monthly invoice can be quite large. It is advisable that the client manager responsible for controlling the project audit the time charges for accuracy.

Occasionally, an audit will reveal time charges for "supervision", charged by an officer, or partner, of the consulting firm. It is necessary to verify that the person charging "supervision" time was specified for this duty in the initial project proposal. Sometimes these charges are justified, sometimes not.

Consulting firm partners and officers usually charge a number of fee days to the jobs run by subordinates under their direct management. In effect, these officers are required to show that a budgeted amount of their time each year is billable and has been charged to clients. Usually, this time is charged under the category of "job quality supervision", or some other time category, and these charges are expected to be equal to a percent of the partner's or officer's compensation (usually 30-50% of his base compensation).

The proposal agreement between client and consulting firm should state clearly who will provide overall supervision of the project and why he is qualified to provide the supervision. In most firms, this overall assignment supervisor also signs the final report to signify his approval of the report contents and conclusions. Many times the officer signing the final report is the "bait man" who sold the project to you in the first place. He may, or may not, have added value to the work of the assignment, and it is up to you to make that determination.

INVOICING AND PAYMENT CONDITIONS ARE FAIRLY STANDARD WITH CONSULTING FIRMS

The invoicing and payment terms are part of the proposal agreed by the client and the consultant. Consulting services are professional services, as are services provided by a law firm, and are handled in largely the same way. Small, highly qualified firms have to face the bureaucracy of the payment procedures in larger, and sometimes not so large client companies, and can suffer cash flow problems because of it. To relieve this exposure, fee pre-payment conditions are usually made a part of proposals by the consultant.

Consulting services in recent years have been provided on the basis of daily or monthly fees, or on a monthly retainer. They have been taken in the form of cash bonuses, equity shares, or a percentage of results for achieving cost savings. There have been payment variations, based on performance, (more common in factory or functional cost improvement projects, such as inventory reduction), which have been included in proposal agreements. As a rule, however, consulting assignments are paid on the basis of a daily fee plus expenses.

It is usual practice for the consultant to require pre-payment, up front, for part of the agreed fee total, but rarely exceeding one third of the total fee estimated in the proposal. Even when the consultant is paid at the end of the assignment for achieving cost reduction targets, there can be a requirement for pre-payment of part of the expected results. Final payment for achieving cost saving targets should be paid after audit confirmation of the cost savings.

Where a long-term involvement by a specialized consultant to top management is needed (usually for product technology, or to develop confidential business strategy for the Chairman), there is usually a guaranteed, minimum retainer which is billed monthly.

The consultants working on an assignment for you are temporary additions to your organization and their invoices should be treated as an addendum, in principle, to your salaried management payroll. Just as the client must pay his salaried personnel on time, the consulting firm must pay its staff on time also. There is nothing more likely to sour a good consultant-client relationship during a critical assignment, than unjustified and seriously overdue payments.

AUDIT THE EXPENSE CLAIMS BY THE CONSULTANT

You must be careful in auditing job expenses to be sure they are charged to you at the actual cost to the consultant. Watch for, and refuse, mark-ups for administrative handling for travel expenses (transportation arrangement handling fees), and such things as special materials and publications purchased by the consultant for use on the assignment. Materials and publications necessary for the assignment work and charged by the consultant become the property of the client and should be documented and deposited with the client at the end of the assignment.

You should insist that the monthly invoice include a summary showing the main categories of expenses for each consultant.

A responsible and circumspect consultant will not saddle his client with excessive expenses, but it is up to the client to specify and control the luxury hotels and the class of air travel to be used by the consultants.

These rules should be spelled out in the conditions of the proposal. Clients—apart from government agencies—do not usually ask for the individual expense vouchers supporting the expense charges on the invoice. The consultant often works more than one client assignment during a month and individual expense vouchers show which clients are charged. The identification of other clients is confidential. There is a modicum of trust expected from a professional firm, and a brief, one page summary of the expenses is usually all that is required. If audits reveal improper charges, the client would then ask to review the individual expense vouchers.

The case of the hidden hat

Years ago every New York and Chicago consulting firm observed a strict dress code. Conservative suit, white shirt, subdued tie and a soft hat were the uniform for client visits. The hat was mandatory, all year round. Mr. Jim Allen, a founder of Booz Allen & Hamilton, was a congenial man, but a stickler on dress code.

On one client visit, Mr. Allen was to be accompanied by one of the newer consultants from the legal staff. A car waited at the office lobby for the trip to the client and the young consultant waited at the door for his Chairman to arrive. When he saw that his companion was without a hat, he told him to go back to his office and get it. The young man said he didn't own a soft hat. Mr. Allen looked at him in disbelief. "Get in", he said. "The driver will stop down the street where you can buy one."

They arrived at the client premises with the young man wearing a beautiful, sixty- five- Dollar Borcellino. When he was told he had gone a little overboard on the hat, he said it was the only one he could find that was his size.

The next Monday, the consultant turned in his expense voucher, which listed one hat in the miscellaneous box, as a charge to the client he had visited. On Tuesday his boss called him in to say he could not approve the hat expense, because it could not be charged to the client. The young consultant didn't complain, although he thought this was an undue imposition.

On each of the following two weeks he submitted his expense voucher, with the appropriate client charges, for approval, and they went through without question. When he saw his expense reimbursements in his month-end check, he remarked to the colleague who shared the same office "I guess he couldn't spot the hat".
It was an improper charge to the client—but it happens.

CHAPTER EIGHT

CONSULTANT "TYPES"

Snowman

A wide variety of consulting "types" have appeared on company doorsteps, over the last forty years and many of these can be shown on the billboard and described for the novice client.

- The "Bird Dog"
- The "Silver Tongued Front Man"
- The "Clothes Horse, "Snowman"
- The "Expert"
- The "All-rounder"
- The "Analytic Master and Problem Solver"
- The "Mole insider"
- The "Junior Birdman"

From the book of experience, we can provide an apt and somewhat tongue-in-cheek description of these few types of consultants before they arrive in your reception room. Before we begin, it is well to remember that consultants primarily active in client business development have a built-in ambivalent character—that is to say, they are tuned to be one thing to you and something else to the next potential client. It all depends on the requirement for developing and closing a sale.

THE "BIRD DOG"

The expression *"Bird Dog"* goes back to the 1950's, and refers to the person doing cold calls at companies that do not know him or his company's products or services. He is charged with *"sniffing out"* sales possibilities, identifying them and turning the information over to a business developer, or senior salesman who is specialized in the industry, technology, or market involved.

The *"Bird Dog"*, or *"sniffer"* as referred to here, is usually a junior consultant who is presentable and familiar with the overall services of his firm. He is armed with brochures and a three minute, audio-visual presentation and his objective is to set the stage for a visit with the appropriate company executive from one of the firm's senior consultants, or business development specialists.

Some of the large consulting firms assign a *"Bird Dog"* to each of the senior business developers. This *"sniffer"* works at his task long enough to know the potential clients in his area (by geography or industry), and waits for an opportunity to be assigned to work on a client project. The *"sniffer's"* performance is measured by the number of doors he opens for his boss, the business developer, who can award him bonuses based on resulting job sales. The *"Bird Dog"* is chosen for his appearance, his tenacity, his initiative, his ability to articulate and his understanding of when to say "I don't know—but I can find out from headquarters", when faced with an unfamiliar situation or complex question.

The very large consulting firms—sometimes referred to as *boutique consultants*—promote themselves for work in almost every industry sector and do not limit their activities to work in any one or two industries. With a very diverse client and industry base, there is constant need in the larger firms for the *"Bird Dog"*.

SILVER TONGUED FRONT MAN

This character is the man the "Bird Dog" usually works with. He is the epitome of a man presented to "know something on any subject at hand". Most clients, when they look and listen closely, may find him to be more shine than substance. He can offset that impression by having a senior consultant, specialist, or technically-oriented colleague with him for support, and to field the more substantive questions that the client may raise. There are, however, some *Front Men* who are the exception, and they are actually knowledgeable and capable of dealing with the substance of many subjects and industries they approach. These rare individuals usually have many years of consulting experience in a broad range of client assignments in several industry and management areas.

This is the person assigned for developing and selling new business with new clients, either in one, or several industry sectors. He is one of the "*locomotives*" or "*rain makers*" the firm needs to keep moving into new business territory to sustain growth and is most often a Partner in the firm.

Business development with the firm's established clients, is mostly carried out by senior consultants who are highly experienced in the client's technology and industry sector. Additional, or "*add on*" business with current clients is mostly dependent on the substance of previous work carried out, and the *Front Man* is usually not involved in those assignments.

The Front Man is quick on his feet, is personable, articulate, displays a sense of humour, is a master at presentation—and, when the questions get tough, very capable at obfuscation. He is unabashed when it comes to dropping the names of well-known private, public and science figures and is quite often trained in law. By natural selection, he has been attracted to a later career in the political arena, working with elected, or appointed officials in public office, where his talents are admired.

THE "CLOTHES HORSE", AND THE "SNOWMAN"

There are always a few of these very conspicuous types in the consulting profession. Sartorial splendour, or practiced *charisma,* sometimes substituted for any quantitative or qualitative knowledge and experience in consulting, that this type should have been gained by carrying out demanding client assignments. More often than not, these types are Partners in or owners of the consulting firm. Experience has shown that this sartorial type is found throughout the world in large, medium and small consulting firms.

The "*Clothes Horse*" is quite often the man in the firm who has the "*connections*" usually in a specific industry, or market area. Retired military officers, former politicians and unseated top corporate executives fall into this group of door openers. When the firm is active in public institutions and government administration, front men from these areas are usually present. It is reasonable to believe that the "Clothes Horse", with his connections, may be very useful in areas such as military products, government relations, garments, cosmetics, personal care, advertising and public relations.

Another type, the "*Snowman*", is found throughout the consulting profession as often as he is found in industry and commerce. He is adept at flooding you with PR information on his firm and its capabilities, exaggerates almost everything, and is unashamed at heaping personal compliments on you—the proverbial *"snow job"* approach. The *"Snowman"* is a front man and, as will the kid's winter snowman, begin to melt under the client's pressure to show substantive subject knowledge in the product, technology or industry. To avoid this melt down, the "Snowman" travels with someone who can answer the hard questions posed by the client.

The "Snowman" and the "Clothes Horse", are similar, and somewhat interchangeable, but, on the side of optimism, both are fading types in the consulting profession.

THE "EXPERT"

I have had several individuals presented to me in industry and in consulting as people who are *"Experts"* in very narrow areas of technology, industrial process, markets, or commerce and they have been quite helpful in some client assignments. Good experiences have been had with experts in glass processes, fuel vapor handling, exotic materials processing, product liability and other subjects outside the knowledge of our own personnel. Attorneys often call on *"Experts"* to provide court testimony for their clients and sometimes cases are won on the basis of their input.

Determining what and who is an *"Expert"* can be very difficult and often lead to wrong conclusions about where his, or her, expertise begins and ends. Does the expertise pertain to historical knowledge, current practical knowledge, or sound knowledge and analytical strength in accurately assessing the probability of future trends and events? Frequently, the latter virtue is missing in most of the "Experts" found floating about in industry, commerce and public administration.

"Experts" are usually sensitive and proud of what they see as the value of their knowledge. They can be difficult for the non-expert to deal with and can be very argumentative when their expertise and conclusions are questioned. This should raise a caution flag in your mind, and can be a clear indication of the limitations of the "Expert".

As indicated by the designation "Expert" these individuals charge hefty fees—in some cases $3,000 to $5,000 per day, so it is wise to know exactly what you will get from him, before he starts.

THE "ALL-ROUNDER"

Most consulting firms place a high value on the professional who has a wide range of industry background and broad consulting experience, over many assignments in general management, financial, marketing or technical functions. This *"All-rounder"* is capable of leading consulting teams and is a capable project manager. It is understandable that, because of these attributes, the *"All-rounder"* is in short supply and becoming more so each year.

Efforts are made to recruit the *"All-rounder"* from positions in industry and commerce and subject him to the training required for a consultant, as specified by the consulting firm. This approach has been only partially successful, due to short-sighted consulting firms insisting that the individual hold an advanced degree. The MBA requirement, eliminates a large majority of the experienced and best talent available.

The *"All-rounder"* is recognized immediately when he starts the client work. He is a communicator and organizer, a solid performer, a team leader, logical in his conclusions and approach to the problem, and is bound more by facts than hear-say and speculation. This does not imply that he is a work drudge. He will be found to have imagination, be innovative and take initiative when demanded.

Consulting firms have a high rate of turn-over with "All-rounders" and lose them to the clients who have been exposed to them.

ANALYTICAL MASTER, PROBLEM SOLVER

This is the consultant type you want assigned to your work project to operate between the people collecting project field data and the project manager, providing analyses and solution alternatives to be evaluated by the project leader. The team leader will draw conclusions from information provided by the analyst to be able to present you with problem solutions and provide practical and realistic recommendations.

This *master analyst and problem solver* type is primarily an inside man, providing data analysis by computer and presenting his findings to the rest of the consulting team for discussion and evaluation. He may be working only on a specific part of the overall client problem, one that fits his special knowledge in a particular functional, product or service area. He might be a specialist in database management, logistics, materials management, quality assessment, or financial and cost models, associated with mergers, acquisitions or divestitures.

You could describe him as the man in the back room being fed information who is digesting, processing and evaluating it for use by project and team managers who design and present conclusions and recommendations to client management. He is the key, *nitty-gritty* member of the consulting team in many complex client assignments.

Although he is an essential part of the team, he is a backroom operator, and rarely makes stand-up presentations to the client.

THE "MOLE" INSIDER

The *"Mole"*, is a member of the consulting team designated to seek out ways to identify follow-on work for running projects, or to identify job possibilities at subsidiaries, other divisions, or other functional departments of the overall company where the current consulting contract is running.

This type is found in large consulting firms that have long-term assignments, running in large organizations which involve large teams of consultants actively designing and installing systems. The *"Mole"* can, for example, be connected to teams that are contracted for large database management projects in large, multi-national corporations.

The *"Mole"* must have ample opportunities to move about in all the client's organizations, and he takes pains to meet and build relationships with managers throughout the company. The client knows him as a member of the consulting team, but his team responsibilities on the assignment are usually left vague enough for him to have significant time for "sniffing" out potential new jobs for which he can offer proposals. The client should be aware that the time the *"Mole"* spends *sniffing*, is not legitimate fee time.

Areas with long-term, large projects where the *"Mole"* is used effectively, are government departments and agencies (i.e. IRS, DOT) and military establishments, aerospace agencies and very large, multinational corporations in the automotive, petroleum, chemicals and mining sectors.

The "*Mole*" can be compared to the "Bird Dog", except the "*Mole*" is more senior and more experienced and works only *inside* existing, established client organizations.

"JUNIOR BIRDMAN"

This is an overly eager and ambitious junior who gets assigned to the consulting team and can, if you are not careful in reviewing the consulting firm's staffing selection, aggravate the members of your company staff. Fortunately, not all juniors create problems, but you should be on your guard against having a "*loose cannon*" suddenly appear aboard your ship as a result of periodic, consulting team rotation. Neither the consultant, nor the client, welcomes an element that will disturb the smooth relationship between them.

The "*loose cannon*" affect of the junior is usually due to his/her lack of experience in handling client staff during functional or systems audit interviews. Tactless criticism of client staff and indiscreet handling of data and information are the most common causes of problems and usually come about when the junior is not properly supervised and kept in line by one of the more experienced senior consultants.

The client staff can be easily put off by the 24 year old "birdman", who postures as a professional with 15 years management experience. Equally irritating is the junior who is not properly prepared and must be taught, by the client, the basics of the company's business, product, or technology, and who then presumes to make off-the-cuff, strategic recommendations to client senior staff.

You are doubly unfortunate when, as a result of the "*bait and switch*" tactic, a consulting project team of mostly junior MBA, "*birdmen*" or "*birdwomen*", has been landed on your doorstep.

The consulting profession, by-and-large, is made up of a collection of normal, unpretentious, industrious, conscientious and educated people of average to high intelligence. Through the consulting firm's careful selection of candidates, the training provided the candidate under experienced consulting professionals and through constant performance review of each consultant, you should expect the individuals assigned to your project are competent for their tasks.

The described "types" while slightly exaggerated, are real, and you may run across one or more of them in your management career, if you haven't already had the pleasure. You can, regardless of your industry or functional area, expect more often to meet consultants who are both colorful and competent, but your responsibility is to be able to determine that the level of competence outweighs their colorfulness.

CHAPTER NINE

EXPECTATIONS—AND RESERVATIONS

You now have a reasonable idea of how consulting firms operate and what you can and cannot expect from them. Consultants are not descendants of *Merlin the Magician*, and they are not always one hundred percent correct in the conclusions and recommendations they offer in solution of your problem. The consulting profession would have slipped into oblivion if they were not far more often right than wrong.

The professional consultant, after long work experience, knows there is no magic formula, nor is there one standard approach that he can apply to solving his client's problem. The computer systems specialist, for example, understands he cannot apply a *packaged*, standard system to fit his client's requirements without making adjustments and modifications that take into account the peculiarities of his customer. This holds true in all consulting assignments, in all planning, organizational, strategic and operating function areas. *For the client, or the consultant, to think otherwise is to invite problems.* No matter how many times the consultant is faced with a client problem that he thinks is a duplicate of one, or several he has solved before, he inevitably discovers something, or many things, that proves the problem, this time, to be different.

HAVING CHOSEN THE CONSULTANT, EXPECT HIM TO UNDERSTAND YOUR PROBLEM AND BE ADEQUATELY EXPERIENCED AND QUALIFIED TO HELP YOU FIND SOLUTIONS

If all the proper preparations have been undertaken to select him, you must maintain trust in his ability to provide valuable service.

You, as the client, must take the consultant into your confidence in all aspects of the assignment you have given him and expect him to be discrete with the information you provide him in his work. If you feed him faulty or misleading information which he has no way of validating on his own you cannot expect the best results. A case comes to mind where the consultant was charged with developing a business plan and market strategy for the chairman of a client company, but was kept in the dark by the head of research and development about a company division's important new product development projects. Success of these projects would require a new focus on company technology, markets and financial resources. The result of the assignment was misleading for the chairman, who had also been kept in the dark about the developments.

The consultant is occasionally exposed to turf conflicts within large corporate conglomerates and he must tread cautiously in dealing with client officers who are secretive, phobic, or are power and image megalomaniacs. You should expect the consultant to keep you informed of problems he encounters and expect him to be experienced enough in large and in even small companies to deal properly and honestly with those things that would impact the validity and reliability of his work.

The consultant, on the other hand, is due the support and confidence of the client's top management when projects of a strategic nature are involved, and you should expect him to call the client's attention to the lack of either.

YOU SHOULD BE PRUDENT AND HOLD A CERTAIN AMOUNT OF RESERVATION WITH THE CONSULTANT'S CONCLUSIONS

The consultant is an independent entity engaged in providing objective observations and conclusions to problems you have asked him to investigate, evaluate and hold out solutions. His findings and solutions deserve to be considered carefully, but with a certain amount of reservation, no matter how large or prestigious his firm may be.

The experienced consultant does not expect to have one hundred percent of his recommendations implemented by the client—on average, only half are ever implemented. Sometimes the low percent of implementation has to do with the intervention of internal *turf wars*, delays due to the corporate preference for *consensus, or committee* management, intended to insulate executive managers from absorbing full risk responsibility for decision making. Implementation is sometimes delayed, or made unnecessary, because of technological changes in the products or marketplace. When the consultant has provided an implementation plan and strategy for his recommendations they have a better chance of acceptance and action by the client. The implementation rate in smaller companies, when the recommendations are practical and realistic, is usually higher.

Reservations about the conclusions and recommendations of the consultant are normal and justified and should be carefully scrutinized and validated before agreeing to their implementation. In most cases the conclusions and recommendations are based upon validated facts that alone may not be subject to question. The reservations usually arise from the interpretation of the factual data given by the consultant, particularly when it is widely divergent from the company line, or direction of thought.

The conclusions and recommendations of the consultant will, in some companies, but mostly in large companies with large staff structures, provide a feeding ground for sceptics and a stage on which a *posturer* can perform for peers and superiors. This is not unexpected by the consultant and the wise professional can deal with it.

In summary, expect the best from the consultant you have chosen, but have some modicum of reservation when he presents his findings, conclusions and recommendations. The following case is an example of the need for caution by a small company, before accepting and implementing change recommendations that would put it at risk from imprudent action.

Case of the tube products company

We were called into the Detroit headquarters of a large client and told they had serious problems at one of their plants in Indiana. The plant manager had hired a local consultant to solve production quality problems that were causing complaints from their auto company customers. The plant was in a very rural area and suffered an annual manpower turnover of almost 35%. The consultants were in their first year of business and mainly worked in production methods and standards setting. After two months of study, they recommended repair and maintenance programs for some of the equipment and proposed redoing the piece work standards to provide higher incentive for the workers to produce better quality. They neglected the high turnover problem and offered no recommendations in that regard. Their report was sent to Detroit headquarters for review and to approve the new standards work.

The President had misgivings about the recommendations and gave us the report with instructions to go to the plant, do a more comprehensive study of the problems and come back with some practical and reasonably quick solutions.

We sent two consultants to the plant and quickly discovered that the first consultant firm was correct in its assessment of the bad condition of the machinery and equipment, but they had missed the main problem. The high turnover of plant workers was due to the boring and repetitive work on production lines, coupled with the frustration of repetitive machinery, equipment and tooling failures. The majority of the workers were women with children and when child-care was not available, they were forced to quit work. The work environment was oppressive due to the heat generated by several long brazing ovens and also was a contributor to high labor turnover in summer months. These conditions were not conducive to worker attention to quality. Most of the tube- cutting machines were out of use, due to the plant manager's decision to contract that work out to a local shop with automatic tube cutting machines. We discovered that the contractor was the uncle of both the plant manager and the purchasing manager.

Our consultants prepared a plan for the replacement of the production lines with a series of work cells that would provide job enrichment and more incentive to produce good quality. The plan called for replacing the old brazing lines with higher-speed equipment that captured the heat and re-circulated it to cut the cost of natural gas and to provide heat in the winter months. The piece work incentives were removed and standards and production bonuses were installed for the work cells and the brazing lines (there was no labor union at the plant).

Several new automatic tube cutters were installed and the work that had been contracted out was brought back, providing jobs for workers displaced from the old production lines. Training in the new systems was provided for floor supervisors and staff workers.

A flexible work schedule was worked out for the women workers with children and a small day-care and play center were constructed in an unused part of the plant, where workers could leave their children while at work and could visit them during break periods.

The labor force was reduced 20% by natural attrition, the quality problems were minimized and the sales per employee increased by 23% over the ensuing two years. Annualized savings, in the first full year of the new cell system, in reduced hiring costs, reduced product returns from customers and higher worker productivity was $850,000 for a plant with a $35,000,000 turnover.

The consulting cost over an 18- month period was $290,000.

The President was correct in his belief that the solution to the problems at his Indiana plant required more than merely resetting work standards and incentives.

CHAPTER TEN

LOOK BEHIND THE FACADE

The large majority of consulting firms in North America and Europe are regional in their scope of operations. Some may provide services in one major city market, while others service a wide region. Most small European firms serve only in their domestic market and don't penetrate beyond their language area. A handful of large consulting firms operate internationally through offices in several countries and have most language capabilities required for each country market. All of these firms, large and small, international and domestic, strive to build an image that will attract prospective clients to their services. Sometimes, the image presented to clients and prospective clients doesn't always match the quality of the services performed.

With the many presentation tools and techniques available to consulting firms and other types of service companies, it is much easier, and less costly, to build an interesting illustrated and verbal facade to put in front of the client. The advent of the internet has permitted small and large consulting firms to present themselves instantly in multiple markets which were formerly approached only via bulk mailing, expensive advertisements and infrequent exposure in business and professional journals and periodicals. Some of the web sites are masterfully designed, innovative and accurately portray the services and capabilities of the firm presented. Others are misleading.

The best way to avoid being bamboozled is to discount the beautiful web sites, the glossy advertisement, the gratuitous mentions in national business magazines—and follow the steps for selecting your consultant as presented in earlier chapters.

EXTRACTING WHEAT FROM THE CHAFF

It is wise to recognize that most consulting firms employ salesmen, or use their officers and partners that are adept and skilled in presenting their services to entice you to buy. Selling an intangible product such as consulting services is a difficult and demanding task and very few people within a consulting firm do it well. Generally, the people who do business development, as it is commonly called, and are successful at it, rise quickly in the hierarchy of the firm and earn ample financial rewards. The value of these people to the consulting firm is great, but their value to the client is usually minimal, because they rarely are involved in the work of a client assignment. These same people may show up again, to present the conclusions from a work assignment the consulting firm has completed for you. Some of these sales "types" were described in chapter eight.

You must be both prepared for, and capable of sorting through the latest (and contrived), buzz-words, power-point presentations, dog and cow charts and statistics, to which you will be exposed by the consultant (all part of the so-called dog and pony shows). Usually, but not always, you will find the consultants who are most qualified in their field make the best presentations. The best are short, clear, use plain language and show a minimum of the detail used in arriving at the conclusions that are being presented. Details are left for reading in the consultant's final, hardcover report.

Sometimes, the key consultant used in the assignment is not the best showman and someone else will do the stand-up presentation, leaving the key man to provide the backup for client questions. This tactic is perfectly acceptable— if the presenter is not there to joke, dance and sing as cover for weaknesses in the deliverables agreed to in the proposal.

Poor presentations are usually too long and too detailed to maintain the client's complete attention and often show a lack of the consultant's appreciation for the value of the client management's time—and it may also indicate weakness in the consultants conviction in the conclusions.

When new concepts and theories are presented, avoid being submerged in extraneous verbiage. When you see this happening, tactfully call it to the consultant's attention and see that he gets to the point– using plain language.

Occasionally, presentations are made to an audience that the consultant mistakenly believes is completely familiar with the technical details of his work and the methods of his analyses. Technical and analytical approaches do not succeed when the audience is made up of managers not familiar with, or interested in technical details, and are interested only in the rationale of the consultant's conclusions.

Be impatient with the consultant who speaks in acronyms and cryptic buzz-words to a general management audience when presenting ideas, concepts or theories. This approach may be perfectly acceptable when speaking to an audience of specialists in the subject technology, but inappropriate for a generalist or financial top management when the objective is to gain agreement for large capital investments.

The former Chairman of ITT, Harold Geneen, was a master at blowing away the *chaff* and getting quickly to the *wheat* of presentations made by prestigious consulting firms and, for that matter, presentations made by his own business unit executives and staffs. He insisted on having facts, without *fluff* and conclusions that defined a clearly designated action plan—and he always received what he demanded. The consultant, or manager, who couldn't provide quick and plain answers, or who *fudged* answers, stood on dangerous ground with intelligent and astute clients, the likes of Harold Geneen.

You should look beyond the often pretentious facade, presented by the consultant, quickly discard the *fluff*—and get to the meat and bones of the problem solution, the system, or the new concept for which you are paying him a large fee. Discourage presentations that report on assignment progress or conclusions, but which really serve the consultant's objective of laying groundwork for new, or *add-on*, work assignments. Understandably, every consultant wants to perpetuate his service to a client, but the client, not the consultant, should determine the need and appropriate time for these discussions and overtures.

Be wary of the *Front man, Snowman* and *Mole* for they can soak up your management time with business development talk and presentations. The man, or woman, you want to hear most from, is the consultant leading the work assignment for which you have contracted. The quality of the work provided in the assignment is the trigger, or damper, for determining whether or not the consultant should be offered a new assignment. As one long-time client and owner of a large company liked to tell me "If a consultant can talk-the-talk, he has to be able to walk-the-walk".

LOOK FOR HUMANISM IN A CONSULTANT

People are the most important resource in any organization, whether it is in the field of manufacturing, marketing, logistics, banking, insurance, or research and engineering. Because managers and employees influence a company's success or failure and since they are affected by and react differently to changes, the consultant should have enough understanding of human nature to determine the weight the company's human resources should have in any equation developed for solving client problems.

Be wary of hyped approaches by firms that have developed a computer model as a *magic bullet* for use in developing strategies and problem fixes. I have often found that computer models do not address the humanity aspects of building a productive and successful business unit, so the client should not rely on them solely.

I have observed over the past forty years the discouraging growth of "*corporate de-humanization*", and the discomforting erosion of management skills in leadership and concern for motivation of subordinates and employees. This erosion has mostly taken place in larger and less in smaller organizations. These are a number of reasons for this trend.

- Many managers of large organizations have come up through an "electronic" environment, an environment that minimizes human interaction, limiting it to contact by e-mail, voice-mail and telephone, or video conferences. Skills in human interaction are not well built within these limits.
- Extreme pressure to grow and *manage profits* has required executives to focus on strategy and numbers management at the expense of the time and effort needed for improving skills in people management and leadership. Quarterly profit management was a tactic taught at the business schools of prestigious universities starting in the 1950's and gained wider acceptance in the 1960's when many company acquisitions were made with equity shares, the value of which were maintained or pushed up by quarterly results.
- Managers at all levels of most large organizations have relatively little training and experience in the motivational and team leadership aspects of their role as managers.
  Evaluation and development of subordinates has been coldly formularized and left to human resources managers to administer. Rarely is time allotted for executives and managers to have one-on-one meetings with subordinates.
  To save time, executives rely on large dinner meetings, sports outings, or *culture nights* as a form of group, do-it-yourself exercises in team-building. These are poor alternatives to the more time-consuming, and more effective, individual approach to personnel motivation and development.

We know that executives and top managers are much averse to suggestions that they lack inter-personal skills—so, this is a subject the consultant avoids, or treats very carefully. The recognition that this skill is a very important aspect of management development must come from the very top of the client organization, along with programs and means to bring about that development.

Many more reasons for the erosion of inter-personal skills can be cited, but the main point to make is the need for your consultant to be aware of the importance of the human condition. When the assignment you have given a consulting firm involves organizational adjustments, or major structural changes, you should look for a team that includes some senior consultants with heavy experience in team building, project management and sensitivity skills.

Dating from the 1980's, we have had an increasing number of clients ask for project management assistance, mainly because of their lack of in-house personnel having team leadership and project management skills. Often, these clients are involved in new product development and engineering projects, or in the organization and start-up of new manufacturing, or support operations projects. We have been able to fill most of these temporary client needs by drawing on our roster of senior managers and engineers having strong team leadership skills, people who were given early retirement in their mid fifties and who are attracted to the challenges of consulting. Many came to us during the *"make way for the young managers"* syndrome that afflicted America and Europe during the early 1980's, and most have become valuable members of our staff and the staffs of other consulting firms.

CHAPTER ELEVEN

IMPLIED VALUES—HONESTY AND INTEGRITY

He has honor if he holds himself to an ideal of conduct though it is *inconvenient, unprofitable, or dangerous to do so.*

Walter Lippmann, 1929

Integrity without knowledge is weak and useless, and knowledge without integrity is dangerous and dreadful.

Samuel Johnson, 1759

The offering of a professional service implies that he who provides that service will serve under a banner of honesty and integrity. No profession is exempt from any one of these three standards of performance, and to fail in any one is to cast away the mantle of professionalism. How contemporary the quotations from Lippmann and Johnson seem to be, in light of today's business environment, at least as the environment is defined by a few executives in the modern corporate culture.

As strong believers in capitalism, my colleagues and I know that the corporate scandals of recent times are aberrations in an otherwise body of thousands of honest corporations and corporate managers. The unfortunate truth is that these failures of trust seem prevalent mostly in very large corporations and damage the interests of hundreds of thousands of shareholders and the security of thousands of employees. The fall-out from these large-scale aberrations is loss of trust in both the corporations and the investment community. Consequently, many well-run and trustworthy companies, including a few of my clients, have difficulty raising funds for product development and growth.

Consultants do not seek out corporate corruption and management misdeeds, but they occasionally encounter both during their careers. How they deal with these situations in connection with their work is an indication of their professionalism.

BLINDNESS TO IMPROPRIETY BETRAYS INTEGRITY

You can demand and expect the consultant to use complete discretion in respect to your business activities, both during and after completion of the assignment he performs for your company. For him to do otherwise, resulting in damage to your competitive position and interests, would be grounds for termination of his services. The professional consultant, however, has an obligation to uphold his integrity and social conscience while serving any client.

When engaged in work with your managers for the development of business plans and strategies, or engaged in functional audits, as part of operations improvement programs, the consultant is usually exposed to financial and accounting data of critical importance. Client improprieties, discovered during an assignment cannot and should not be dismissed by the consultant, particularly when he sees a pattern of continuity in the incidents. If the client's improper action is shown to be a single incident of error, or faulty judgement, the consultant should not treat it with a blind eye and is obliged to call it to the attention of client management, together with reasonable recommendations for safeguarding against future incidents.

Observing repeated impropriety, which may or may not be systemic, or may be triggered by specific company motives, should oblige the consultant to immediately call this situation to the attention of client management. When the client will not recognize or agree with, issues raised and fails to take immediate corrective steps, the consultant is expected to inform his client of any exposure to potential or impending liability as a result of failure to address the problem. When the client again avoids taking corrective action, the consultant should give notice of his withdrawal from any and all assignments given him by the client. To do otherwise would exhibit a lack of professional and social integrity.

It is not unusual for a professional team of highly experienced consultants and auditors to be engaged for years inside a large client organization such as Waste Management, Cendant, Sunbeam, Xerox, Lucent, Enron and WorldCom, and to be heavily involved in issues of operational, financial and strategic importance. It would be unreasonable for anyone to believe that, over an extended period of service, the consultant would not become partly or completely aware of the correctness, or incorrectness of the company's activities and, hence, aware of management's treatment of shareholder interests. For the consultant to ignore a client's patently improper management of shareholder interests solely to assure continuity of a professional fee is, as held by Samuel Johnson, *dangerous and dreadful.*

The vast majority of management consulting will be found somewhere, between the overly righteous *Miss Goody Two-shoes* and one at the very bottom who prostitutes himself for the objectives of his client. Determining where any consultant lays on this integrity scale is not easy and cannot always be determined through checking his client references.

Standing on good principles, when dealing with and serving clients must be the rigid posture maintained by the consultant. In the view of some clients, however, this rigid adherence to principle may be interpreted as an extreme attitude for a consultant to have. Managers, solely interested in promoting their own self-serving agenda look upon a consultant's strong stand on principles as a lack of flexibility. And, not infrequently, a client will seek out a consultant he thinks is pliable enough to provide independent but supporting confirmation for a weakly conceived plan, a faulty operating strategy, or an overly optimistic market forecast. It is in the best interests of the consultant to avoid a client with these objectives, lack of integrity and with this type of mind-set.

On the other side of the ledger, it is, without exception, in the best interest of an objective, open-minded and well-managed company to avoid pliable consultants whose principles are set in something less than concrete.

The following case from our archives illustrates a proper consultant's response to recognized managerial improprieties.

The case of the "borrowed" technology

A wealthy, mid-western businessman contacted us to look into the commercial feasibility of a new technology owned by a company he had invested in on the East Coast. Based on the company President's claims about the large potential market for the technology, when applied in an automotive product, our client and some of his business acquaintances had invested several million dollars. The company President had showed our client a report from a consulting firm that praised the company's development work and forecast very optimistic market potential for the product the company intended to further develop and produce. Our client had not bothered to contact the consultant who produced the report to inquire about his qualifications in the area of automotive products.

Our client introduced us to the company President and made arrangements for myself and two more colleagues, to spend a few days examining company operations, the product and estimating the downstream financial needs for manufacturing. What followed was a dance with the devil.

The company President was the head of a large family clan in the town, and ran the operations from a converted, old, tobacco warehouse. His Executive Vice President was an attractive woman, half his age, who headed planning, finance and marketing. She was assisted by a secretary and receptionist (an aunt of the President), and by a male bookkeeper, somewhat in his eighties. The shop was run by a garage mechanic, a welder and a metal forming worker who, together, manufactured and installed the product on forklift trucks for a large company in the state. The product incorporated both electronics and special materials to clean engine emissions. The President had had a small, California laboratory run tests to certify that the technology worked. We were shown the test certificates and when we asked for someone we could speak with at the laboratory, the reply was that the laboratory had since gone out of business.

We were wined and dined by the President at the most luxurious waterhole in the county and were invited to spend a weekend at his mountain hunting lodge. We declined the invitation. The President drove a Mercedes 500, but his Exec. V.P. was driving a more economical BMW 735i. The President's aunt drove a Cadillac Eldorado.

We examined the financial accounts for the preceding two years and found numerous payments to special consultants and extremely high travel charges for business trips to California, New York, Las Vegas and New Orleans to attend conferences, including two trips to London and Paris for business seminars. The books had been audited at the end of each year by a local CPA. This man was, as it turned out, the brother of the beautiful Exec. V.P.

The President, unabashedly, informed us that he had to raise at least five million dollars to push the technology into production for industrial vehicles and trucks. When asked if he had a business and financial plan, he said he was under the impression that we were there to put one together for the company. We left him with the word that we would reflect on what we had learned and get back to him later to discuss the business and financial plan.

Back in Detroit, we did some rapid research to confirm what we thought was true about the technology involved and found that it was a patented technology held by a company in Italy. We contacted the Italian company and were told that they had not licensed the technology to anyone in the United States.

We reported all of this information to our client and advised him not to invest more money in the company. We also advised him to take his losses as a learning experience—it would be useless to litigate. The President had all the assets out of reach, the money was gone, and the only ones who would benefit from litigation would be the attorneys.

*   *   *

This case was not the worst of its kind we have encountered when working on behalf of unwary investors, but it was an example of a situation the client, by being judicious, could have avoided.

CHAPTER TWELVE

BUILDING LONG-TERM RELATIONSHIPS

The best and enduring relationships between a consultant and his clients are built on mutual trust and the provision of quality service. With some clients, the confidence and trust is strong enough to reduce the formality of the proposal process for less than complex assignments to an E-Mail exchange of service requests and letter proposals. Long-term, complex assignments, no matter of how long and solid our relationship with the client, are always based on client agreement to a formal, detailed proposal as described in Chapter Five.

More frequent changes in the top and second level management of large and medium size companies have interrupted some of the long-term relationships between established consultants and their clients. The interruption is mainly due to the appointment of new executives in the client organization who favor other consultant firms with whom they have had previous experience. Few consultants live under the delusion that their relationship with a company will be unending, and their experience reveals that client change is the only certainty in their profession.

A displaced consultant can sometimes offset his loss of a client when a friendly executive leaves for a new position and provides work assignments for him at the executive's new company. This shuffling of consultants is common and disturbing and provokes constant business development by the consultant, to maintain a budgeted business volume.

The client who has a long and exclusive relationship with a consultant or consulting firm may be exposing himself to a weakening of the independent thought and counsel he needs from an outside source. Long and familiar relationships between client and consultant have a habit of rubbing some of the client's corporate and business management culture into the consultant's staff—and this is not a desirable development when fresh, new approaches to the client's problem solutions are sought. In other terms, the consultant's perspectives in all areas of his involvement should be wider than those of his client.

Some very large consulting firms perform several millions of dollars of fee work for their largest clients, and enjoy this to the exclusion of equally qualified and competent consultants. As unpopular as the idea is to the very large consulting firms, the client should invite different firms from time to time to compete for new assignment work on an equal basis with his long-time, established consultant. Had this approach been taken at Enron, WorldCom, Swissair and other organizations of recent note, there might have been earlier warnings, and some chance to avoid part of the troubles that befell them.

Building and maintaining a good relationship with your consultant is certainly important, and should continue to the degree that he remains an independent and objective influence. He can remain important to you in many functions, but will be effective only when he remains at arms-length from the intrigues of your company politics. He has to work closely with your management and staffs, but must be able to resist any restrictions on innovative thought, imposed by your corporate culture.

Some relationships between consultants and individual executives are built on shaky ground when the executive is weak and living with paranoia in fear of their managerial weakness being exposed. Often a consultant is called on to act as a barrier between his client and other company executives and to make backroom decisions for the executive. This is a dangerous relationship and sometimes continues as the executive moves from one company to another, taking his trusted consultant with him. Eventually, the executive's weakness is exposed and his demise is often shared by the consultant. The following case depicts a situation relationship that should have been avoided by a consulting firm and violated just about every rule in the consulting profession.

The case of the "ghost" thinker

An old college chum of the managing partner of a medium-size consulting firm in New York City was elevated to president of a large family-owned group of companies. The promotion had little to do with merit but a lot to do with the fact that his wife's family controlled the business and there were no male heirs in the wings.

The group consisted of ten companies in the food sector and included large bakeries, home baking products, packaged soups, spices, condiments, frozen foods and sugar refining. The new president had formerly managed the sugar refining business. Total group annual sales was $1.8 billion.

Two months after taking his position, the president called his old college chum for help in preparing a new business plan and strategy that would include two newly acquired businesses. His consultant friend asked why he did not rely on his staff to put the new plan together. The gist of the reply was as follows. "Those guys are ticked-off because they were passed over for this job and they are waiting for me to make a big mistake—and to be honest, I don't know enough about the other businesses in the group, but you know about them and I trust you."

This started a chain of consulting assignments over the next three years. The managing partner of the consulting firm was made a member of the advisory committee to the board of directors. The chairman was the wheelchair-bound father-in-law and the board consisted of the president, treasurer, the legal vice president, the chairman's two sisters and the president of the company's main bank, the only outside board member.

It was soon apparent that the president was not capable of managing the group of companies without almost day-to-day assistance from his consultant friend. It did not go unnoticed that all major issues, requiring decision by the president and the board, were first sent for review by the consultant. When new systems and operating procedures or cost reduction and operating processes were required the president's friend got the consulting work. Paranoia ruled the president's office and he seldom met with his division managers, leaving that to his consultant. When he did attend meetings they were large and orchestrated by the consultant, including the wording of the president's presentations. The annual consulting fees gradually moved to one million dollars and stayed at that level for three years.

The company prospered during the next three years, mainly due to the capable management of the division vice presidents. The consultant had wisely left the development product and marketing planning and strategy to the divisions and review by the consultant before presentation to the president and board.

Eventually the morale of the division managers and key corporate staff began to erode as they caught more glimpses of the inadequacies of the president and recognized they were being camouflaged by the intervention of the consultant. Late in the third year of this arrangement six of the ten division managers resigned, citing weakness of top management and their isolation from the president and the board of directors. Although the consultant and the president were aware that there were no strong successors for most of the division managers, the consultant had not made strong recommendations to develop the next lower level managers.

The Chairman and the board called in each of the resigning division managers to state their cases. The president and the consultant were next on the docket and asked to explain the reasons for the exodus.

The upshot was the recruitment of a new president by the board, moving the president back to manage the sugar business and informing the consultant that there would be no extension of work for them after the current work was completed. The most serious blow to the consultant was his college friend's suicide, three weeks after his demotion to division manager.

CHAPTER THIRTEEN

TECHNOLOGY CONSULTING SERVICES

Your approach to the use of technical consultants should be guided by the same principles used in selecting general management consultants, except that strong emphasis must be focused on the technical experience of both the consultant and the consulting firm.

Research and development and product design engineering services are a separate service category and are not included in technology consulting services as described in this book.

Technology consulting services, for the most part, include provision of field and desk research in the following areas:

> *Materials research*
> Product technology research
> New technology assessments
> Technology application forecasting
> Economic feasibility of new technology
> Research on competing technologies
> Engineering project management
> Engineering productivity improvement
> Product development strategy
> Sales engineering support

There are only a few firms that successfully provide both general management and technology consulting services internationally. These firms are usually industry specific, and specialize in one or two industries, such as energy, automotive, communications, computer, chemicals or pharmaceuticals. Consulting firms of this type are usually in a better position to assist companies develop and apply products and technologies in foreign markets where the companies do not currently operate.

AN INTERNATIONAL TECHNICAL SERVICE CAN EASE PRODUCT QUALIFICATION
IN EUROPEAN MARKETS AND PROVIDE PRODUCT SUPPORT

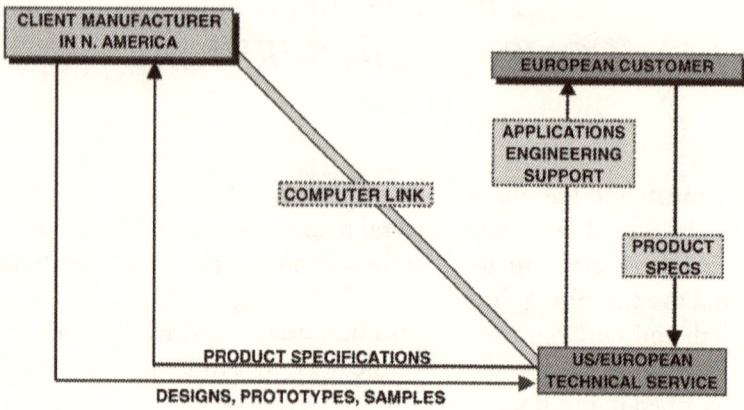

In addition to the technology consulting services listed in the box on the previous page, full-time applications engineering can sometimes be provided for the period between product design and product start-up in the country where the client's customer is located. This important service can be provided when and where the client needs heavy pre-sales product support in close proximity to the customer.

OPEN-ENDED OR RESTRICTIVE CONTRACTS

Technology service consultants usually work within the bounds of the product or technology assignment specifications provided by the client. These types of assignments can be short, or long-term (six months to as long as two years) and the proposals covering them can be open-ended, or restrictive.

OPEN-ENDED CONTRACTS

Open-ended contracts are usually for long-term assignments lasting more than six months and involve project management or technical research teams that support the client's total design-development effort for a new product.

This work is usually provided on a man/day fee basis and may, or may not, be carried out on the client premises.

Contracts to provide sales engineering and product support at foreign locations, as liaison between the client's engineering department and the client's customer, are usually open-ended.

RESTRICTIVE CONTRACTS

Restrictive contracts are used for projects where the consultant works independently of the client technical organization, to produce research data on materials, technology, competitor product assessments, in support of new product or product revision. This work is usually carried out on a fixed time and cost schedule agreed with the client.

Many companies, particularly in the automotive industry, have found that small, technology consulting firms working on a fixed fee budget and time plan with financial penalties can usually show higher productivity than the client company's own engineering function. The key element here is to be sure the consultant has the knowledge, experience and personnel to get the work done by the required deadline.

PROJECT MANAGEMENT FOR NEW PRODUCTS

Technology consultants are often called upon to provide senior consultants to lead a client's product development team. This service is becoming more frequent as more of the client's senior technical managers leave the company or retire, and younger managers are not properly trained and skilled in project team leadership.

The length of its *design- production cycle,* and the cost accumulation between these two points, can make or break a company in today's high-technology business sectors. Shortening this cycle is difficult and achievable, but demands excellence in co-ordination, co-operation and managing the flow of timely information between the company's engineering and its other management functions. Getting there requires well-defined and adeptly applied project management skills in organization, procedure and cost control.

You should be aware that not all project management contracts have ended in success, so there are cautions to be taken when qualifying and selecting an outside service to carry out this important management task. The following list is not exhaustive, but points out some key danger points in selection of a technical consultant.

VETTING THE TECHNICAL CONSULTANT

- Ask for the references from the consultant's former and current clients who have used him or her for technical, project management, or project support functions.

- Verify that the consultant has knowledge and experience from previous work in the products, material, or process technologies, subject to his assignment.

- If a team of consultants are involved for both technical, desk research and field research in market and economic feasibility analyses for forecasting applications, be sure that each member of the team has the appropriate training and experience for his or her individual task.

- Be sure that the consultant is well-aware of and understands the current and the emerging technologies that compete now, or will eventually compete, with the new products, or technology, you have under development.

Reputable international firms that provide technology consulting services in your particular product or area of technology, will have staff members who have published papers and studies that involve the areas most significant in your project. Researching sources of technical papers in your area, will often provide leads to the identity of an appropriate consultant.

TECHNICAL SURVEILLANCE SERVICES

Most companies do not have a good grasp of current product and technology developments taking place in their industry and among their competitors. We have found that while some clients are somewhat informed about these things in their domestic markets, they lack intelligence on foreign markets and foreign competitors. Inadequate intelligence in these areas has lead some clients to accepting faulty market forecasting and has led them into costly investments in fading products and technologies.

Technology consultants can design and carry out market and technology surveillance programs for their clients that run continuously for a designated period of time. These programs produce an initial surveillance study that is up-dated each three to six months. The cost is usually much lower, and the comprehensiveness much greater, than when the task is carried out by client company staff. This is especially true when looking at many foreign markets and competitors.

The expandable surveillance report normally covers:

- the published and otherwise known product developments being carried out by competitors,
- technology developments taking place at research institutions,
- changes in competitor market shares, new company entrants as competitors,
- significant changes in key technical management of competitors.

These surveillance programs are usually carried out by a team of technical and market consultants assigned to do the initial study. The follow-up, intelligence work is usually assigned to a smaller team (one consultant and one or two researchers), who make up-dated presentations to the client every three to six months. In the interim, significant changes and developments in technology, competitor products and markets are reported as they occur, without waiting for the scheduled reporting dates.

One of the advantages of using an international consulting firm for surveillance work, is their ability to gather intelligence from many language sources and provide a synthesis in the client's own language.

Finding a consulting firm in your industry that provides both general management and technology consulting services will usually produce more credence in market forecasting and analyses when the firm thoroughly understands your product technology and competing, or emerging technologies. Assigning product and market strategy development to a firm that specializes in your industry area should make more sense than assigning your automotive engine development strategy to someone who specializes in the cosmetics business. But we have seen companies make stranger decisions.

A RESOURCE FOR ONE-TIME PROJECTS

External, technology consulting services, provide a ready resource for avoiding the time and cost of hiring additional, full-time staff for projects which are either one-of-a-kind, beyond the load capacity of the permanent staff, and/or have critical completion schedules. When the project is completed, there is no excess staff to dispose of and the consultants are on call for any follow-up required on the work they have done.

The caution for the client resides in seeing that the consulting firm can provide continuity of service, during and after the assignment work. The firm should be large enough to be able to replace any project team members who leave before the work is completed.

CHAPTER FOURTEEN

CONSULTING IN ANOTHER WORLD—THE PUBLIC SECTOR

We would be remiss to neglect a much different sector of consulting where many hundreds of millions of dollars are sometimes wisely and effectively spent—and where, also, the money is sometimes spent poorly.

Consulting relationships in the private sector are reasonably straightforward. A senior company executive senses a need for a qualified and objective outsider to look at his strategies, approaches to markets, his competition, operations systems, or some other problem. The chances are, this executive has used consultants before and begins a face-to-face dialogue with an officer of the consulting firm. Sometimes, this dialogue and the consultant's broad experience, changes the executive's perception of his problem and how it should be approached.

The consultant will normally want to do some plant, or office walk-arounds, talk to managers, review financial and operating statements and systems. With this done, he submits a detailed proposal as described in earlier chapters.

THINGS ARE DIFFERENT IN THE PUBLIC SECTOR

Comparatively, there is a night-and-day difference in consulting for the public sector.

What do we mean by "public sector"? This "administered" world starts with small towns and cities, goes to county, state, regional and national agencies. The big-time organizations include international agencies of sovereign states, such as the United States Agency For International Development and aid counterparts in most other developed countries. It includes multinational organizations, such as the International Monetary Fund, The African Development Bank (ADB), Asian Development Bank, and other acronyms (FIAS, MIGA, UNCTAD), and literally hundreds of other entities.

Because the public sector spends billions of dollars for consulting services each year, most, if not all the large consulting firms in the United States have operational offices in Washington, D.C. They serve many U.S. government agencies and departments and also the large, international funding agencies, including the World Bank and USAID, where both of the latter have continuing need for advisers, technicians and consultants for developing country projects.

The mission of all these agencies, particularly those at international level, is to do good things for others. But, by their very natures, the "do-good", projects of these agencies often involve very complicated and bureaucratic systems, procedures and approval authorities. These are rooted deep within their organizational hierarchies and work up the elaborate chain of command affecting project funding and approvals. Many people are included in this chain except, unfortunately, the actual recipients of the assistance funding, and the consultants who will carry out the work. They do not become directly involved until after critical project decisions are made. When the project assistance has been carefully defined and budgeted, only then will the recipient country be involved, and only then will the consultant be asked to submit a proposal for providing specific deliverables.

It is the rare consulting firm that questions the project approach, the staffing, the timing or the deliverables—even the firm's experience tells them that the project is flawed in concept, or approach. The two parties with most to contribute to project design and execution, those who will have to implement and live with the results, have little or no input into the planning and formulation process—the process which often determines whether or not the targeted goals and objectives make sense and are achievable. The dialogue process, fundamental in private sector consulting, never enters the picture.

The missing Link

I wish they'd told me how to turn it on!

DEVELOPING COUNTRIES DON'T ALWAYS GET QUALIFIED AND PROFESSIONAL SERVICE

In a number of cases we have found serious deficiencies in the experience and quality of people selected for World Bank and USAID projects. This first-hand observation has been made by experienced consultants who have managed large, third world projects, not funded by World Bank or USAID, but funded by the host government itself, and often by large, private organizations. The community of foreign specialists and consultants working in any developing country is usually small in each country, and it permits frequent, social interaction and opportunity for professional assessment.

The title of "Expert", "Specialist" and "Consultant" bestowed on the individuals showing up for third world projects is sometimes justified—but only sometimes. In too many cases, usually to the detriment of the host country, any one of these designations far exceeds the quality and experience of the individual on which it is bestowed.

The developing countries most in need of highly qualified, experienced and professional assistance don't always get the people they require, even though the funding has been made available to provide an appropriate level of assistance. The poorer nations are frequently *short-changed* for several reasons, foremost of which could be termed bureaucratic ineptitude. The second reason is the widespread belief that, because the poorer nationals are economically and technologically under-developed, the greatest consulting talents available would be too much of an investment for solving basic and rudimentary problems. In other words, the prevailing wisdom is: "*don't use expensive talent in developing country programs*" The third reason is easily understood. Highly paid, qualified and experienced consultants in industrialized countries are not normally, motivated by altruism and not inclined to accept assignments in under-developed areas, where the pay, living, working and sometimes cultural conditions are vastly different and often present hardships.

Development assistance work in third world countries is, without question, vastly different from commercial and industrial management consulting in North America and Western Europe. This difference, however, is no justification for professional consulting firms to apply a lower standard of professional service. The standards, unfortunately, do seem to be different and the reasons are worthy of definition.

STRUCTURED BUREAUCRACIES

It would be difficult to find someone, no matter how civic-minded and patriotic they may be, who thought of their Government, as anything other than a giant bureaucracy. Consultants who have endured encounters with government officials, systems and procedures find it amply clear that public organizations are more *administered* than they are *managed*—and this condition extends to the large, international funding agencies controlling the selection of consultants for contract assignments in developing countries.

Consulting firms that spend large amounts of time and money developing contract business with U.S. Government departments and the international funding agencies must deal with *administrators* who are quite different from the professional managers they are accustomed to serve in the private sector. This conditions the consulting firm's approach to staffing assignments. For now, we will limit our review of how staffing is done by those organizations funding and administering program assistance for developing countries.

THE USAID APPROACH TO CONSULTING

USAID's manpower budgets are established as part of the annual U.S. Government budgetary process that establishes the number of permanent professionals that the agency may employ. When new priorities or project needs require additional staff, over and above the authorizations, the agency will often recruit individuals from outside, to serve for a specific contract period. Such positions are not "counted" as permanent staff and enjoy only such benefits as are specified in their contract with the agency. These contractors, Personal Services Contractors or PSCs, are not employees in the Civil Service sense, but serve under very specific terms of reference for two or three years. They usually serve within a country Mission, occupy Mission offices and are placed under a specific career officer for supervision. The PSC may be recruited to carry out a specific task, working within the structure of a recipient host government agency. USAID in Washington normally carries out the recruiting and hiring process. The country mission sees the paperwork and gives it's approval, but rarely interviews candidates.

We can summarize USAID's several categories for obtaining consulting assistance:

- Personal Assistance Contracts
- Contract bids and awards
- Indefinite Quantity Contracts

The personal assistance contract is used for someone who will work inside the local USAID Mission office, or will work for a long-term on a USAID client assignment, for example a local investment authority, a national bank, a government ministry. In this case the USAID client has no say in the qualification and selection of the consultant, or the consulting team—that is done by the USAID Mission office. In this category, there may be several persons working under personal assistance contracts, at a USAID Mission, who can be assigned to a work team for a client assignment.

The contract bidding and award process applies to projects requiring several consultants to be supplied by a USAID approved consulting firm. In this case, a statement of requirements is provided by USAID to several consulting firms, that are required to make a formal proposal which includes a package of profiles describing the individual consultants being offered by the firm. If the consulting firm is awarded a contract, they will staff the assignment from the listing in the proposal. In these cases, the local government recipient of the funding for the project has no say in the qualification and selection of the consultants that are eventually assigned. Again, the qualification and selection of the consultants and specialists is undertaken by USAID, and rarely with the USAID client review or input.

USAID has a third category of contract called Indefinite Quantity Contract (IQC), which is used when the agency knows they will need various consultants over a period of time, but do not want to go through the bidding process every time they need a new or replacement consultant. This IQC is awarded to a consulting firm and the Mission Director can call on the firm for people without having to go out for bids. To our knowledge, there is very little vetting by the Mission Director of the consultants offered up by the consulting firm. Again, the USAID client has practically no say in the selection of consultants for his project.

Through their management consulting arms, major auditing firms have been active making proposals for both projects and IQC tenders. They have found it profitable to pass work along to specialized sub-contractors, which use consultants with relatively low daily fee rates. McKinsey & Co. and Booz Allen & Hamilton, the two U.S. revenue leaders in international consulting, have not actively sought project or IQC work, because they don't wish to assign personnel that are not on their permanent staff. USAID, in any case, will not normally pay the high daily fee rates McKinsey and Booz Allen charge their private sector clients.

Consultant quality control and overall project supervision is extremely difficult when part-time people, not employees of the consulting firm, are assigned to overseas projects through one of the sub-contracting body shops. Further problems arise from the failure of consulting firms to budget sufficient fees and expenses to do the pre-overseas orientation and briefing of the consultants assigned to the projects. Budget is often not provided for essential, periodic overseas, on-site supervision and quality control by the officers of the firm.

Part of the weakness in the process of vetting and selecting consultants can be laid to a built-in mind-set on the part of both the consulting firm and USAID officials—those who are responsible for the quality and appropriateness of the consultants chosen. Both look upon the developing nation client as being incapable of vetting and selecting consultants on its own. This mind-set seems to persist, even when the client organization is headed by local nationals, educated in the USA and Europe, who hold advanced degrees and have management work experience in highly-developed countries.

THE WORLD BANK APPROACH TO CONSULTING

Recipients of World Bank (WB) funded assistance for long and short-term projects, have almost nothing to say about consultant selection. Consultants are selected, approved and sent out for WB project work by Washington headquarters. A few reasonably well-known consulting firms are awarded WB contracts and supply the project consultants. However, these firms rarely assign their own, highly qualified professionals to the projects; instead, they recruit less expensive personnel through several Washington-Arlington based "Body Shops". In most cases, the bodies proposed have, what appears to be, "qualifications" in the subject field of the project—in reality, the selections are often poor.

We can relate two illustrative cases where the names of the consultants have been changed and the agencies involved have been omitted.

Case One—The National Investments Project

S. Johnson, a senior international consultant with both operational and consulting experience, was retained by a small consulting sub-contractor (a body shop), to undertake a study on behalf of a major, multinational funding agency. The study was to recommend strategic "start-up" guidelines, policies, structure, staffing and budgets for a new national investment project, recently enacted by a host country legislature. The project was urgent and Johnson was asked to fly to the host country immediately, with no time for stopping in Washington for briefings and discussions with those in the agency who had developed the project terms of reference. The people he missed seeing would be responsible for ensuring approval of project recommendations and the follow-on funding for an operational overview of the investment project operations.

Johnson's terms of reference stated that he would have hands-on assistance from three other individuals. The in-country Deputy Director, would assist with introductions, government co-ordination and report production. A senior officer of the funding agency, based in a nearby country, would periodically visit the proj-

ect to review the report draft, prior to presentation in Washington. A Washington-based lawyer of the funding agency would be available to review and counsel, relative to local codes, laws and regulations.

Johnson arrived and reported to the Country Director's office. The Director was unaware of his arrival and had only a vague idea of the project. Johnson asked about the Deputy Director's participation and was informed that he was away on a four-week training program and not available. Had anyone been named from within the host country government to co-ordinate Johnson's work with the appropriate agencies? The answer was no.. The Director was not aware of any such arrangement.

Over the first two days, Johnson prepared a work plan and schedule, discussed and agreed it with the Director, faxed it to the Washington-based legal advisor and the nearby-country associate. The legal expert replied that he had been transferred to Europe and would not be available for counsel. The neighboring-country officer of the consulting firm indicated that getting into the host country was difficult, and if Johnson sent him a copy of the final draft, he would be happy to review it.

<p style="text-align:center">*   *   **

This case is probably the worst of a worst-case scenario, but the very complex nature of the funding agency's project design, consultant selection and Washington's management of the local, in-country, co-ordination and control process were a major factor in the resulting confusion. The confusion did not go unobserved by the host country.

The case may be indicative of too many of the assistance projects underwritten by large funding agencies and it reflects poorly on the professional consulting firms that undertake them. The consulting firm responsible for this project failed to manage it.

We have seen that the critical element in successful, private sector assignments is direct and early discussion between the client's senior executive who will guide the study, inform other executives where appropriate and will be responsible for approving and carrying out the consultant's recommendations, and a senior member of the consulting organization, who will be responsible for oversight of the firm's team of consultants. These two key players normally establish and agree the terms of reference, the scope and schedule of the work and the expected results, in terms of the "deliverables".

This fundamental was totally inoperative in the above case. Nobody in the agency's headquarters knew exactly who in the recipient country should sign off on the study scope and objectives, provide guidance and assistance during the work, approve recommendations and be responsible for shepherding the proposals for approvals through the local government network. The funding agency failed to keep the in-country team informed and was unable to deliver on the services of other supposed contributors to the project. The on-site consultant was lost in the middle.

Our experience confirms that this "disconnect" situation is all too common in international agencies with authoritative and heavily staffed head offices. The approach is to drive programming from the headquarters, rather than through their on-the-spot staff in the field offices.

There is a glimmer of hope though. The WB and others have come to see the fundamental weakness in their traditional, Washington-driven programming and are now beginning to delegate more decision powers to the field offices, but the "Washington knows best" and "Not invented here" attitudes will take a while to fade away.

USAID has, on the other hand, traditionally delegated a great deal more responsibility to their field offices and has, over recent years, groomed a cadre of professional and capable, career Mission Directors, backed by appropriate resident specialists. But even here, it has been literally impossible to involve the consultants who will do the in-country work in the process of project design, thus effectively preventing them from gaining any up-front understanding of the organization and people with whom they will be working. This exclusion of experienced inputs is, to say the least, unwise.

The USAID Mission Director's first meeting with the assigned consulting team, and the first meeting between the consultant and the local government agency involved, will usually take place after the team arrives to start the assignment. By that time, it is much too late to change project goals, objectives, scope of work, or timing, and it is too late to make changes in the size or composition of the consulting team. Case two illustrates these major problems.

Case Two—Staffing with disconnected free-lancers

A multilateral agency retained two teams, each with three consultants, to carry out two studies. Team one was to study development of a national investment agency and team two was to conduct feasibility studies for the creation of duty free zones and investment estates. Both teams operated independently, working under the supervision of two different government ministries. Both teams had almost no official project relationships, even though the project work of both teams was very much related. None of the consultants had worked together before, and none were employees of the contracted consulting firm—all were free-lance operatives.

The head of the Free Zone team was located in one city, but the other two members of his team were in another city. It was apparent that the personal relations between the leader and his two team consultants were poor, and communications were even worse. Serious discord within the team became evident to the supervising Ministry and they were ordered to "pack and go".

The second team worked out of the same office in the parent Ministry. Communications were facilitated by daily face-to-face contacts. But there were problems here as well, mainly lack of team building leadership and control of the consulting process.

The team leader was very intelligent, possessed excellent verbal and human relations skills and was a highly qualified specialist in investment promotion. Unfortunately, he had no experience inside a professionally run consulting firm, and was unable to organize the team and assign responsibilities. The second team member was equally well qualified, but had never participated in an overseas assignment. Both the team leader and the second consultant, while fluent in spoken English, English was not their first language. They both had limited skills in organizing and structuring the English language reports. Only the third team member had experience as a professional consultant.

*   *   *

The problems in this case were very apparent—if anyone from the contracted consulting firm had taken the time to look. In fact, during the several months involved, no permanent member or officer of the U.S. consulting firm, nor anyone from the international funding agency that was paying the fees, came on-site to the project to review work being done. The results? The Ministry client cancelled the Free Zone project in mid-stream, and the work of the second team was of questionable merit.

The main point in our experience with these kinds of projects is that the people who approve the consultants never see the warm body, and have no idea of the importance of solid consulting credentials. The consultant chosen may be a perfect dud, but his curriculum vitae or CV said he once worked in the field under consideration. The agency officials who send consultants to developing countries may have some text book familiarity with chicken and egg production, but in most cases they have no idea about organizing to help someone in a hardship area establish a chicken and egg company.

Objective observation indicates that pointing the finger of blame only at organizations such as the World Bank and USAID may be pointing it in the wrong direction. Why? Because ultimate responsibility for qualification and performance of the people assigned to projects, when all is said and done, belongs to the consulting firm that made them available for the work in the first place.

THE UNITED NATIONS APPROACH

Most of the selection of consultants by the UN is handled in New York City through an organization called UNOPS. This organization prepares and advertises tenders in publications such as The Economist, asking for individual and company proposals for assistance projects. The UN client receiving the funded assistance does sign off on the accepted proposal, but it is doubtful that he has much say about the makeup of the consulting team, or its individual members.

IN THE PUBLIC SECTOR, INDUSTRY AND FUNCTIONAL EXPERIENCE ALONE DOES NOT A CONSULTANTMAKE

The failure to match client country needs with consultants competent to carry out a given work program underlies many of the questionable results that bilateral and multilateral agencies achieve under their current consultant procurement practices. These agencies seem not to recognize that specific industry or functional expertise is but half of the story. Demonstrated success in the practice of consulting is the other half, and equally if not somewhat more, important. The only way for a consultant to qualify, should be to have worked in a professional consultancy, or from having gained experience working under the supervision of a recognized professional.

An individual may be the best expert in the world on a given manufacturing, process, or computer system, but his lack of experience in the process of consulting is all too often the cause of small and large disasters. This is particularly true if the individual is the team leader and is not subject to supervision in the field by one of the consulting firm's seniors.

CLIENTS IN DEVELOPING COUNTRIES SHOULD PARTICIPATE IN THE APPROVAL OF THE CONSULTANTS WHO WILL IMPACT THEIR FUTURE

It is incorrect to assume that all of the recipients of assistance paid for by the large funding agencies are not capable of assessing the qualifications and experience of the consultants that will be assigned to a project that is important to their economy or social infrastructure. This, unfortunately, is the assumption held by funding agencies and consulting firms that manage and staff projects.

During the 1950-1960 period, very few third world nations had educated and trained human resources from which they could draw on to cope with their many development needs. By the 1990's many local managers, some professionals, and a great number of technicians had returned to their home countries from higher education and training in America and Europe. Through our contact and work experience in a number of developing countries, we have found ample, local capability, in all economic and industrial sectors.

The general attitude of funding agencies persists. To put it in their words: "We are putting up the money, we know exactly what they need, so we will decide who works for them." Developing countries should speak out in opposition to this mind-set and should insist on participation in all phases of the selection and monitoring of foreign consultants.

CHAPTER FIFTEEN

THE VALUE OF SENIORS IN CONSULTING

Since the middle 1980's an increasing number of senior managers with vast and varied experience in many functions and technical disciplines have come into the consulting profession. The many have joined smaller consulting firms that specialize in a particular industry or area of technology. Our firm has welcomed this valuable human resource and has trained many for consulting assignments. Without exception, all of these senior consultants have performed superbly for our clients.

These senior *"re-treads"* find homes in the smaller consulting firms mainly because most are *too experienced*, do not have MBA degrees and are of no interest to the larger consulting organizations.

As more of these managers are induced to leave industry for early retirement, many at the ripe old age of 55, some will hang up a consulting shingle and find it to be a lonely and competitive life. Those who wind up in one of the small established consulting firms find a rewarding, collegial environment where their special skills and long experience can be employed for the benefit of many clients. Over fifty percent of the consultants in our firm are between fifty and sixty five years of age. They are active, innovative and valuable contributors to our own growth and to the needs of our clients.

When it comes to job security for managers and workers over 50, the United States and most countries in Europe have, since the middle 1980s, been depicted as "throw-away" societies. There is little doubt that over the past decade there were an increasing number of managers with vast and varied experience in many functions and technical disciplines, appearing in company-sponsored out-placement programs. As paradox, many retired executives and managers are being called back to industry to provide leadership to management and project teams lacking in experience. To repeat an earlier observation, many younger managers have risen through an electronic environment with limited requirements for personal interaction and many have little experience in the team building and leadership requirements of management. A case from our archives might help to illustrate this point.

The case of the engine turbo project

During the down-sizing rage of the 1980's a large engine manufacturer gave several experienced design engineers and some key engineering managers early retirement with attractive pension provisions. The company was left with mostly young talented design engineers who could support the current range of engines and could manage the long-term development of new engines. This proved not to be enough capability when the company suddenly needed a quick change in engine design strategy at the end of the 1980's period.

Competition and market demands required a quick up-grading of the company's mid-size engines by adding turbo-charging. This required solving some complicated design problems for each engine category. The company soon discovered it lacked project management leadership to meet the critical changeover deadlines. They contacted our firm for assistance.

One of our senior engineering colleagues (70 years young) was highly experienced in engine design and turbo-charging and was the designer of a widely-used engine used in the auto industry for over twenty-five years. He was the right man to lead the project.

The assignment required that we provide three design project managers; one for each size and category of engine. The project managers had to be both design experts and project management trainers for the younger engineers. The project tasks would have to be completed in parallel, within one year, to have engines on the market within 18 months and before a foreign competitor introduced its new line of engines.

The young engineering managers at first resented the company chairman's decision to bring in outside help. We held a general meeting to introduce our colleagues, discuss the problems and the approach to managing the three engine projects. We were able to point out many problems that would confront the design teams and illustrated how they had been solved in the past. In a short time the company engineers were working in smooth concert with our project managers and were benefiting from a series of off-hour training sessions.

Each of the three design projects and the manufacturing engineering portions were completed ahead of schedule. Most problems encountered in the projects were shown to be the equivalent of problems our consultants had solved in the past and this fact alone saved months of tail-chasing in working out false or dead end solutions.

The company chairman hosted a dinner for the engineers and our colleagues and gave our firm credit for completing the projects ahead of schedule and under budget. With our agreement, he awarded each of our three project managers a special bonus and awarded an additional special bonus to our firm.

WE JUST DON'T SWITCH-OFF AT AGE 55

I'm gone

We were not born with a switch, nor has anyone had a switch implant, that shuts us down at age 55, or 60, or 75. Although modern man's life expectancy increases, his active employment career does not. One colleague observed that, "If this trend continues, there might be more people carrying consulting business cards than there are managers to read them." This may be an exaggeration, but clients will begin to see more senior consultants on assignment over the coming decades.

Industry cannot afford to have all these valuable human resources go fishing—they should be going hunting instead; hunting for problems to solve and new things to create. Retirement is not a red light; it should be a green light for starting a new era of productiveness.

Othmar Ammann "retired" at 60. He then designed:

- The Connecticut and New Jersey Turnpikes
- The Pittsburgh arena
- The Throgs Neck and Verrazano bridges
- Dulles International Airport

Paul Gaughin "retired" and became a world famous artist.

Winston Churchill won the Nobel Prize for Literature at 79.

Experience does count heavily in success and when you look for a consulting firm, find one that includes a reassuringly high ratio of seasoned, mature professionals, heavily experienced in your business, industry, or technology area.

CHAPTER SIXTEEN

WEIGHING IT ALL UP

Big business has become grist for the media mill in both America and Europe. Corporate executives no longer have the comfort of acting behind a curtain. They perform center stage, under the spotlight—with auditors and consultants entering on stage left, to play supporting rolls. At the end of each act, the audience rewards good performers with applause, and responds to the few greedy and bad actors, with *boos, jeers*—and sometimes jail sentences. Everyone out front leaves the theatre hoping and expecting that they will not see these bad actors again.

The roll of the consultant is also undergoing more public scrutiny and justifiably so, in many cases. Some, who abandon professional integrity, will disappear as a consequence. The great majority of professionals that perform competently and maintain their integrity will not lose the trust and confidence of the thousands of the honest managers and companies they serve.

Capitalism is binding its recent wounds and will eventually heal itself. The great cultivators of business and industry will eliminate weeds and bring back the flowers.

PERFORMANCE REVEALS THE CONSULTANT

Members of the consulting profession are a selected group, screened from a population of well-educated people. The screening usually filters out everyone but the most qualified people to serve demanding clients. The filtering process can reveal education, intelligence, experience and a reasonable assessment of the psychological makeup of the consulting candidate, but only through work assignments and proper supervision, can an assessment be made of his or her true character, work ethic, human interaction skills and integrity. The same criteria must be applied for assessments of the consulting firm.

Relatively few management consultants have long-term careers in the profession. Many leave for management positions in industry. This does not mean that consultants that stay and make long careers in the profession are not highly capable of serving in industrial positions. Most stick with it because consulting satisfies their need for a wide range of challenges and/or because they move up quickly in the management of their firm.

Whether any consultant or consulting firm is qualified to assist the client is for the client himself to determine. We have attempted to outline the cautions to be taken in this selection process. Just remember that every consulting service can be rated on a scale of from 1 to 10 for experience, quality and performance, so be judicious and choose carefully, especially if you want to contract with someone on the high end of the performance scale.

Both public and private sector bodies should "*invest*" in consulting services with the intention that they will yield future benefits. Highly experienced and professional consultants as well as industry managers, for that matter, are not abundant and are expensive. When well chosen, they can save many times more than the amount invested in them. Fees for a consultant are high and usually cannot be "bargained", unless a long term of service is expected. Consulting fees are only difficult to negotiate when the economy and the market for assistance is expanding. That means clients can wear their *bargaining hat* when the bottom of the market has dropped out, and the economy is in the doldrums.

Many companies, in their approach to becoming "*lean and mean*" have thinned their staffs to the extent that the remaining personnel have difficulty coping with the important and time-consuming "one-off" problems or projects that management wants covered. Diverting managers from day-to-day problems and projects of a "one-time" nature can be expensive in terms of lost sales, delayed product launches and missed profits. Using qualified consultants to fill the gap can be an alternative. If your problem needs an urgent solution—a decision to set the stage for a consultant is probably equally as urgent.

Management must remember that even the most experienced and qualified consulting firm will sometimes face problems for which it cannot quickly find solutions. That caution will be announced up front, so don't expect miracles— and beware of the consultant who purports to have the magic power to perform them.

Pay particular attention to the composition of the consulting team you let in the door. If the consulting work is going to impact human relations and performance in your company, be sure the team includes senior people who have had long experience in managing human relations. Don't expect good results if the team is made up mostly of *electronically-grown* and case-study insulated MBAs.

The following case compares the sterile and calculating approach to a more humanized approach to solving a client's organizational problems.

The case of the humanized merger

We were engaged by a large, family-owned company to assist in the reorganization of a major division being merged with a recently acquired, competitor. The objective was to reorganize in a way that would minimize the loss of jobs for the employees and managers of both the mother-company and the acquired company. Both companies supplied pumps, valves and metering equipment; the client supplied the water utility and natural gas sector and the acquired company supplied the petro-chemical and automotive filling station sector. Both companies were quality leaders in their field.

The client had acquired the competitor through the services of a large, well-known consulting firm which had indicated that after the merger at least 25% of the combined headcount of 5000, should be eliminated. This firm was well known for its "robotic" or "slash and burn" approach to headcount adjustments following mergers and acquisitions. The approach did not sit well with a family which had run its businesses with as much interest in the welfare and security of its employees as it did in growth and profitability.

The company Chairman believed that our firm would take a more humanistic approach to his employees and managers than would be the case, if the larger consulting firm were given the assignment. The client's goal was to maintain a high level of production efficiency and increase the pace of new product development in both product lines, in order to maintain employment for the highest number of workers and managers. Headcount reduction was to be managed through normal attrition. Together with the key managers, we had one year to accomplish the task.

Through a series of presentations introduced by the company Chairman we described the company goals, its approach to achieving them, and explained our role in the process. The presentations were made to mixed assemblies of managers and workers. Managers and workers of the mother- company were more confident that the merger would be painless than were the managers and workers in the acquired company, who knew little of the character of the owners.

During the next ten months we helped form working groups, made up of both employees and managers in each functional area to study and develop plans for consolidating the Personnel Administration, Finance and Accounting, Marketing, Sales Engineering, Sales Administration, Quality Control, Product Research, Development and Engineering (RD&E) functions. During this period the only jobs lost were those vacated by people retiring, or by managers and staff who left for jobs in other companies.

The RD&E functions of both companies were only partially consolidated, with the R&D functions being merged, but with a Design Engineering and a Sales Engineering function remaining in each of the two product locations. Coupled with investments made in new product development for new market sectors, and increased marketing and sales effort, only 9 of 120 jobs in RD&E and Sales Engineering were made redundant.

By bringing back manufacturing work that had been out-sourced, and with the additional business volume generated by accelerated product development, and with extra sales effort in all product lines, it was necessary to make only 370, manufacturing operations jobs redundant.

The result of the co-operation between the managers and the employees was a 415, headcount reduction, instead of the 1250, recommended by the larger consulting firm involved in the acquisition. Two years after the merger, sales per full-time employee had increased 32%, over the combined sales per employee of the two companies before the merger. The best result, in the eyes of the family owners, was the continued good employee/company relations and the peaceful relations with the company employee's union. There were problems, frustrations and arguments during the whole period, but experience, keeping eyes on the company's goals, and the humanistic approach to each problem by both the company managers, the employees and the consultants brought general satisfaction.

Six months after the completion of our assignment, the client and the company union presented us with a commemorative award for our work and efforts in helping to preserve jobs throughout the company.

*   *   *

Deciding whether or not to hire a consultant, and finding one that is best for you is a serious matter. Look carefully behind the glossy facade of the big players before you choose—sometimes what lies behind is mainly smoke and mirrors. There are many smaller consulting firms of excellent reputation and quality that should be considered in the selection process by the largest to the smallest client companies.

When you have recognized a problem that would justify the use of an independent service, go through the self-preparation process described earlier and make a decision for or against. Procrastination may enlarge the problem you have to solve.

*   *   *

The source of the following has been forgotten but it seems a good note on which to close.

> Sometimes the decision to do nothing is wise,
> but you can't make a career of doing nothing.
> Freddie Fulcrom weighed everything too carefully.
> He would say. "On the one hand.....but then, on the other."
> And his arguments weighed out so evenly that he
> never did anything. When Freddie died, they carved
> a big "0" on his tombstone.

Freddie

What's the point?

You could say the point is you should *fish or cut bait*. But if you decide to do nothing, you sure won't have fish for dinner.

ABOUT THE AUTHOR

The author is an American, New England-born and educated, with both executive management experience in manufacturing companies in the United States and Europe and international management consulting experience in North and South America, Europe, the Middle East and Asia. He has held senior executive positions in ITT, Bendix Corporation and Sprague Electric Corporation. His career included work in manufacturing plant management, financial management, construction management and marine equipment design and manufacture.

Following work as a factory manager, he spent ten years in industrial consulting devoted to providing economic and industrial planning assistance to developing countries. He was a Managing Associate at Booz Allen & Hamilton International, managing large projects in North Africa, Iran, Iraq, Turkey, Pakistan, Thailand and Indonesia before being recruited for a corporate position in a large international conglomerate. After senior executive positions with three major corporations he found corporate objectives narrow and the lack of intellectual challenge demanded a change in career direction.

He founded a management consulting group in Europe and the USA in 1978 which serves over 350 companies, of which 18 are among the Fortune top 100. The group has carried out over 2500 management and technology consulting assignments, in 35 countries.

He lives part of the year in Switzerland, part of the year in America and does strategic consulting for a few clients, when not writing for publication and sailing in the Buzzards Bay and Narragansett Bay areas.

0-595-26810-2

www.ingramcontent.com/pod-product-compliance
Lightning Source LLC
Chambersburg PA
CBHW030857180526
45163CB00004B/1611